MAN•u•*Script*

THE ETHOS OF MANHOOD

Copyright © 2019, Deborah Williams
Author, Deborah Williams
Illustrator, Toney Designz
Editor, Deborah Williams
Cover Design Assistant & Graphic Artist, Malachi Williams
Forward by Freddie Williams

Requests for permission to reproduce any part of this book should be directed to The Deborah Williams •
D.Williams@QuoniamGC.com

Library of Congress Control Number: 2019911432

Summary: Man-U-script, a collective narrative of 15 Black men speaking man-to-man and man-to-single mom about the realities of being a Black man in America, and the nuances of successfully raising black boys into God designed manhood.

ISBN 978-0-9840289-5-5 (soft cover)
ISBN 978-0-9840289-6-2 (e-book)

First published in 2020 Deborah Williams
Printed and published in the United States of America - 2020

Artist, Toney Designz

This book is dedicated to the man of my dreams; to the man I've loved for a lifetime. I dedicate this book to the man who's been enriched with charisma and endowed with the strength to hold my hand; to the man I've spent my years looking up to, to the man whose very existence says to me 'write on'. I dedicate this book to you ...Black Man.

MAN·u·Script

THE ETHOS OF MANHOOD

Deborah Williams

PREFACE

Man-U-Script was birthed out of a need to know what it takes to nurture a boy into manhood. How does a mother raise a man-child to recognize and eventually realize his purpose as a man in a world that continues to gnaw away at the distinction of masculinity? What exactly is required of me during his development? As a single mother, just what do I do, and how do I do it – whatever IT is?

The day I became a mother with no preparation and little anticipation, I was struck with the overwhelming reality of the weight of my new responsibility. I was raising a Black man-child in a country that maintains a legacy of despising the very essence of who he is, his lineage, and physicality. To compound my quandary, I needed to know how to raise my son to be a man according to God's specific design. So off I went on my quest for answers, direction, and insight from a masculine voice.

I read books and watched videos, starting with Dare To Be A Man by Bishop David G. Evans, Why Men Need Visions & Dreams by Dr. Myles Munroe, and Armed And Dangerous by Motivational Speaker Les Brown. At some point during my search I communicated my mission to a cousin of mine who was incarcerated. To help me, he asked a few fellow inmates to share their perspective on manhood, specifically life as a Black man in America. And so, the letters rolled in. Cousin Elisha Glover, I thank you!

Each man penned his perception of manhood, filtered through raw personal experiences and subjective observation. Letter after letter was replete with invaluable truth-nuggets and painful realities. The common thread that ran through each letter compelled me to explore further.

I sought out men from varied walks of life; Business Professionals, Skilled Craftsmen, Police Officers, and Clergy, men from the Midwest, South, Northeast (specifically New York City), and from the Caribbean, retired and employed. The unique chronicles from these men, coupled with the narratives from the men in prison, seemed to speak as one voice that pointed me to the answer.

So here you have it - **Man-U-Script**, the collective voice of 14 men who dared to share with me, and now you, the realities of what it takes to raise a man-child into manhood successfully.

Also included, a poem by my late cousin Ronald R. Hines; and finally, prose written by yours truly.

Introducing Deborah Williams

Deborah Williams is a writer and mother to a brilliant little boy (in his words – "Big Boy"). She graduated with a Bachelor of Science in Sociology from City University of New York, Baruch College, and held a successful career in Corporate America before embracing her calling to write.

As a woman of faith, Deborah writes to encourage spiritual growth, to ignite the conscious mind, and to stimulate positive personal and social change. Her first endeavor as a published author was "Wisdom for the Excelling Life," a repository of testimonials and morsels of life changing wisdom. She subsequently authored the 'Kids for President' children's book series. She has since launched the MoorBrothers.com blog that serves as an outlet for black men to discuss the nuances associated with being a black man in America.

Art Jones, Photographer

:Follow me:
On Twitter: TheDeborahWilliams@QuoniamGC
Instagram: @ TheDeborahWilliams
Blog: https://www.moorbrothers.com/
Facebook.com/MoorBrothers

Table of Contents

FOREWARD.................……………….................... 1

LEAD ………………………........………... 11

PROCESS ………………………………......... 19

SILENT & SOLITARY…............................. 34

BLACK MEN …………………………….. 37

BLACK IN AMERIKKA……....………........ 45

CHANGE ……………………………….... 51

UN-CYCLED …………………….…....... 63

WAR ……………………………….…....... 73

CHOICE ……………………….…................ 77

SHIFT …………………….….................. 95

FOUNDATION …………….......………....... 101

A FATHER'S LOVE …………......…............. 107

PRESENCE ………………………............... 121

IDENTITY ………………………….…........ 131

MAN-CHILD …………………….…............ 141

I SEE A MAN …………......…..…............. 151

BLACK MAN ……....…………….…........... 155

CONCLUSION …....………….….............. 177

FOREWORD

By Freddie Williams

The idea for this tome was birthed out of the mind of the author, and conceived with two questions: How and what? How does a black woman raise a black child into a black man - a black man of God, in these times where that very designation seems to be haunted, hunted, and hated; in a time where the ideal of manhood has been cloaked in effeminance, draped in violence, adorned with ignorance, or simply erased; in an age where women don't tell their age and men don't act theirs? How does one effectively cultivate masculinity in an environment that has relegated it to hypersexualism, sophomoric behaviors, and aggression? HOW??? WHAT??? What resources, networks, traits, qualities, etc. are necessary elements for successfully rearing this man-child? What will she need to do, need to possess, need to sacrifice to bring him into purpose, position, and power? The author, finding herself tasked with the immense responsibility of raising a precious, delicate black male life, ardently made this inquiry of herself and of the Lord. Resultantly, this stellar work was produced.

I met the author in 7th grade homeroom at West Hollow Junior High School. There were four of us sharing the last name Williams, 3 young ladies and myself. We also shared the experience of being raised and culturalized in Wheatley Heights, New York, the hamlet neatly juxtaposed between Wyandanch and Dix Hills, two distinctly different socio-economic worlds.

The four of us became fast and lasting friends. We each possessed very different qualities and pronounced traits. And of us, Debbie, among other things, was the spiritual compass; quick to laugh, ready with a smile, eager to listen, but notoriously intolerant of crass, debasing, behaviors. Early on, Debbie possessed a weightiness of thought, and a stability of spirit. Though we fell out of touch, it did not surprise me years later when we reconnected, to hear she was a rooted woman of God, a published author, and that she had answered the divine call to mother a beautiful child.

The vitality of her son's future is bathed in her prayers to our Heavenly Father and the concerted outpouring of her gift to write. Having published "Wisdom for the Excelling Life" in 2010, and 3 of her 10 book "Kids For President" series, "Emmett for President", "Jia for President", and "Luke for President"; God seemed to be steering her towards content centered and fixated on enriching children by empowering parents.

Man-U-Script is a transcendent literary product that draws upon the input and insight of 14 men from diverse backgrounds and beginnings, joined by a common thread of belief and the common bond of blackness. It spans the spectrum from poignant to painful, from incisive to introspective, from social commentary to soulful cries. The narratives presented within Man-U-Script vividly and vibrantly utilize the paints from the palette of each man's soul to paint a portrait of manhood. This volume, you will find, addresses several critical issues, all of which are rooted in manhood: What defines and constitutes a man? What role do boyhood issues play in manhood? Each chapter is aptly titled and artfully written, not by New York Times bestselling authors, but by men who have experienced much, overcome more, and stand in their various positions and locations wiser; enriched by experience and empowered by erudition. These rich voices represent a cross section of black American men, chronicling and conveying their stories, woven herein into the majestic tapestry of this book.

In these testimonies a key component to child rearing is revealed: that is, never underestimate the power of presence. This axiom was typified near the turn of the twenty-first century when young bulls (male) and adult female elephants from South Africa's Kruger National Park and Game

Reserve were relocated to Pilanesberg National Park while adult bulls were killed or retained at Kruger, a measure taken to quell Kruger's burgeoning elephant population. What ensued at Pilanesberg was extremely distressing. Mutilated rhinoceros' carcasses were found at Pilanesberg, and as time passed the number of violent killings grew. Upon investigation it was discovered that roving bands of the very juvenile male elephants from Kruger were wreaking havoc. These culprits were not only chasing down and killing rhinos, they were terrorizing other animals as well. Further examination concluded that the absence of adult male elephants was the destabilizing factor in the young male lives, dramatically disrupting their social behavior and impairing their ability to make appropriate decisions. In their natural hierarchy, adult bulls model behaviors and keep the young ones in line. In an effort to curb the crisis, Park Rangers flew in some of the older bulls from Kruger. Within weeks the attacks ceased. The natural world and science confirms that the mature male presence is essential to social development.

I would never be as condescending to compare our humanity to any animal. However, there is a lesson to be extracted from the above. The absence of positive male role models (fathers) is generationally debilitating to individuals as well as to society: 70% of persons incarcerated, 80% of rapists, 71% of high school dropouts 63% of teens who commit suicide, all have a common denominator; they come from homes with either absent or abusive fathers. Literally every social ill and every social pathology can be linked to a deficiency in fatherhood.

We currently live in a society in which 2.3 million individuals are incarcerated. The incarceration rate in the U.S.is by far the highest in the world. Mass incarceration trends have adversely and disproportionately impacted our homes; 1 out of every 28 children has an incarcerated parent. That number becomes 1 in 8 when applied to the

African American child. In the U.S., 40% of children are born to single parent households; that is 76% when speaking of black households. Manhood, men, fathers are absent, incarcerated, ineffective, uninformed, misguided, miseducated, misled, preoccupied. The consequence: generations of suffering, misguided, and maladjusted children.

The impact and absence of a father, a man, in the lives of youth can never be underestimated. Fathers model roles, establish order, and exhibit the methodologies of manhood to their children. The reappearance and reintegration of fathers into our homes and communities would redeem the family (the root of society) and reverse societal ills caused by their absence (over time). A positive role model in a young man's life greatly improves his chances of success later in life.

With a collective voice the men in this book definitively declare that authentic manhood was discovered and revealed to them through their relationship with the Lord, and that the model for men is presented in and through Jesus Christ.

That being said, Black man, as you read this profound body of work, I encourage you to have your mind and heart open. Whether you follow Jesus Christ, Elijah Muhammad, Noble Drew Ali, Clarence 13X, or the prophet Muhammad; whether you study the Bible, the Qur'an, or 120; whether you are beginning at the book of Genesis, Al Fatiha, or Supreme Mathematics; are quoting John 3:16, the 15th Ayat of Surah, or the knowledge degree in the 1-14; there is a thread that binds us. Whether you are in Bed Stuy or Baltimore, Compton or Chicago, Magnolia Projects or Marcy, we need a clear understanding that the survival of our nation, of our people is wholly contingent on our ability to protect, position, and prosper the next generation.

Man-U-Script is a magnificent kaleidoscopic narrative that compels us to instill in our children the assurance that nothing around them, neither poverty nor prestige can accurately reflect the wealth of intellect, imagination, innovation, ingenuity, ideas, and intuition that is inherent within them. Foremost, it is incumbent upon us to recognize and respect the same within ourselves. One cannot give what he does not have or understand, and cannot lead others to where he himself has not the foresight and fortitude to venture.

Black woman, with each turn of the page, you will hear men break their stifling silence; bare their hearts, expose their wounds, and share their dreams. Take heed. The truth is that you have not just nurtured and raised children. You've inadvertently raised adult males who never truly passed into the realm of manhood. You've mothered 28, 38, 48-year-old males, praying that they would one day evolve into the man you knew they could be, were destined to be, that you needed them to be. In these pages you may find your husband, boyfriend, father, or your son.

The book ends with a roll call of esteemed individuals in the realm of Blackdom, and closes with this; "Your name is among them." And it is; along with your sons' names, and your daughters' names, and the names of their children, and so on...

LEAD

WILLIAM BELLE

I think the ultimate joy of fatherhood is to be able to raise a son to be a successful man. I speak from a Christian world view when sharing my perspective of manhood and fatherhood. A Christian world view tells me that a successful man is a man who grows up to love the Lord, to be a good husband, to be a good father.

One of the most successful coaches in the history of football once said that if his son grew up without knowing the Lord and if his son became anything but a man of God, then he himself had failed in spite of the many accolades and great accomplishments in his football career. I stand in agreement with this world-class coach by saying again that a man's ultimate joy in fatherhood is to see his son live as a man of God. At the same time, that joy is tied to the importance of manhood, and that being to lead by example.

As a parent I started out with the belief that you could simply say all the right things to your son, teach him the correct things to do, and then he'd follow suit. Then I matured and discovered that more is caught than taught. I regret not having this insight when I was raising my children.

The lectures and brilliant speeches turned out to be mere lectures, in one ear and out the other. The things that became a part of my son are those things that he repeatedly observed in me; one being my thought processes, be they good or bad. If what he saw was a critical spirit, that's what he caught. If he observed a judgmental spirit, that's what he caught. When I see him doing negative things, I look at myself and recognize that he caught that too, and that's the challenge. He caught more, good and bad, from watching my actions than he did from listening to my words and unpersuasive speeches.

Guiding children is something that's done on purpose. Although you have to be intentional about parenting, the guiding doesn't so much happen with the intentionality of a father's words as it does with how a father operates. We would like to think that it all happens with words and lectures, but the ultimate evidence of guidance is seeing your son walking as you walk.

It's been said that imitation is the ultimate flattery. This rings especially true when you see your son trying to emulate you, particularly when you see that he loves the things that you love. Watching him in his attempt to be like you is an unexplainable satisfaction. I don't think there's a greater joy for a father than to see his son enjoy the things that he enjoys.

The experiences and things that my son and I shared were and still are a great source of satisfaction for me. My son and I would go fishing, attend men's meetings and go on retreats together. I can put it no other way than to say that there was a lot of joy in sharing things and experiences with my son. I'd tell myself with pride, "This is your son. This guy comes right out of your loins." However, the ultimate responsibility kicks in when you realize that your son is trying to be you. I'm the man that he's patterning himself after. If I'm not living right, my son is liable to end up being a mini-monster instead of a man of God.

I think boys want to walk like their father, that is, until they reach the teenage years. The teen years are when a young man seeks independence and tries to establish that he has a mind of his own. In spite of how great a father you are, the opinions of his peers may be more persuasive than yours.

Now, to my daughter I was the model of manhood that she knew growing up. The example of manhood that she saw in our home was to become what she would deem normal, which made raising her an awesome responsibility. When she looked at me she saw hardworking, industrious, and active. She saw a man who loved and took care of her. She saw a man who took care of the home. As her father, I was the primary man to tell and show her how valuable she is. Whether she admired my qualities or not, I was her model of manhood. And like every other girl, she compared men in her life to her father. I set the stage for her husband. When she was looking at men, she was attracted to what was normal and familiar to her, and that's the kind of man she chose to marry. Girls marry the kind of man their father is, be he good or bad.

There were times when I fell short of being the example I should have been when my daughter was growing up. Once struck with the reality of my wrong, I purposely sat down with her, admitted my error and apologized. As a result, our relationship was fortified. The atmosphere was then set where she could come to me with her mistakes without the fear of being judged. If she could trust me with her faults, I could then help to shape her. You can't shape anybody unless there's a sense of closeness. You can't have a sense of closeness, unless there's a sense of trust. And you don't ever have a sense of trust, unless there's disclosure. My confessing and apologizing to her was beneficial to the both of us.

Fatherhood is a significant part of a man's life, likewise the role of a mentor. Whether he grew up with a father or not, when a man reaches a certain level of maturity, he recognizes the necessity to impart life-knowledge to the next generation of men. Having a father in your life or even children of your own is no prerequisite for being an effective mentor. Plenty of great mentors are fatherless and or childless. It's critical for a young man to have someone to mentor him, and that mentor need not be a father.

Over the years I've been able to share the positive aspects of my life, the things that I've benefited from, with the young men I've mentored. In doing so I've found that I get to share more with my mentees than with my own son. In conveying the wisdom gained from my experiences to these young men, I do so without the emotional component that exists between me and my son. I simply share and give solicited information. On the other hand, when advising a son there's often a level of resistance, because a son is striving to be his own man apart from his father; and a father wants to be sure that his son is rightfully representing his name.

Some might think that leading a family, being a model or replica of manhood, and serving as a mentor is a heavy responsibility. But this is how a man is supposed to live. It doesn't take a superman to do what you're supposed to do. Living out one's responsibilities is actually normal. I find joy in handling my responsibilities. For a man leading, modeling, and mentoring is normal responsibility. It's rewarding.

Graphic Designer, Malachi Williams

PROCESS

CRAIG HOLLIDAY

My story starts out like so many others; my mother, a smart, beautiful, strong, hardworking, godly, praying woman, and my father, an abusive alcoholic. The joys of my childhood were misshaped by the infection of my father's alcoholism. On too many occasions I saw, heard, and felt his drunken rage, but could do very little to protect myself. By the age of twelve I decided that I would protect myself by ignoring the pain and the emotions caused by that pain, and then I ran full force to be a better man than my father. I was determined not to be him, and was definitely not going to be a chip off the old block. For all intent and purposes, I was going to run the course of my life as far in the opposite direction from his as possible. But then I had an encounter that changed the course that I had planned for myself.

On the surface I was my father's polar opposite. I excelled in school. I played ball as a star athlete, which took me to and through college. After college I was at the top of my game in the business arena and was still holding it down on the basketball court. By most standards I was doing quite well. By cultural standards I was a pretty good example of a good man. But, then one day I found myself sitting in a state of self-imposed abandonment all alone in my apartment. It was in that weighted silence that I recognized who I'd become. I had become my father - the man I vowed never to be, the man I strived to be better than. Without knowing, I was absorbed in my own self-serving satisfactions just like him. No, I wasn't drinking, fighting, or caught up in any vice. Mine was a warped need for personal success; and his, a deviant craving for alcohol. We were both chasing something that had the potential to destroy us.

Success in itself is not a bad thing. In fact, it's good, but I had it all twisted. I had displaced God as head of my life with the hustle for achievement. I came to the point where I realized who I was and how much this broken man needed to change. I needed God to change me, so I asked Jesus Christ to step in, take over, clean me up, and make me right. Accepting Christ as Lord of my life was the beginning of my walk up the corridor that I call process.

At the beginning of my process I came to the realization that I was an emotionally and spiritually broken man. First, I had to be honest with myself and recognize that there were some things in my life that I wasn't particularly proud of. I then recognized that I had actually become the man that I never wanted to be. I had become a mirror image of my dad's emotional instability. But then I came to the place where I said, "God if You're real, if Jesus is real, I need You to change me." It was then that the fundamental and practical changes began.

Prior to this point, I spent years questioning God's existence. I'd ask myself, if He really did exist could He hear our prayers. Yes, I had a praying mother, but it seemed like the more she prayed the worse things got around our house. It looked like my dad got worse with every prayer. I questioned the very notion of God. Where was He when the situation at home was in such turmoil? If God was listening, why was the tension still going on in our home? Could He not hear my mother's cry? Did He not hear her prayers? But then, for the first time I realized that this God that I had this bent against, this God that I saw my mom worship and pray to relentlessly, this God that I thought was sitting back and doing nothing while my dad got worse; I came to realize that this God who I learned about as a child in Sunday School, He is real. And then, when I arrived at the place where I was face-to-face with myself, I saw my desperate need for God and who He is. I said, "God, if You are real, You're going to have to change me. You're going to have to transform my heart."

I needed God, and by that point I knew it. Nothing that I had previously tried was able to bring me satisfaction. My career wasn't satisfying me. Living with someone and trying to fill the void that way, didn't work. Nothing could fill the hole or satisfy the craving that I had. I had been searching for something without knowing what that something was. I came to the point where I had to actually sit down and say, "Ok, what's driving me? What's the meaning of life? What's my purpose here?" I had to drop all pretenses and get honest with myself. I had to look at how I approached life and recognize that I had some areas and behavior patterns that needed to be dealt with.

Self-examination revealed that even though I hadn't picked up my dad's vices, I had unknowingly acquired some of his character traits. I've since come to realize that not only are we handed the physical traits of our parents, but emotional and spiritual traits pass on to us as well. The characteristics and traits that I was exposed to played out in how I approached life throughout high school, college and into my adult life. Those character traits were the source of my lack of trust in God and my distrust of others. As a result, life left me cold from years of not being able to trust the person who failed to protect me as he should have. I walked around with a coldness that came from a hardness that was birthed out of years of disappointment. On the outside I looked like I had it all together, but there was this war raging on the inside of me. Like everyone else, in order to change the course of my life I had to walk up the long and sometimes painful corridor called process. I had to get alone with God to allow Him to bring about the much needed changes.

After my life-changing encounter with Christ I wanted to be a man according to God's plan, since my own plan had failed. I knew from watching my mother that God's plan is always a sure win. So, from that day forward I opened my Bible to absorb all that I could about manhood according to God's standards, and God surrounded me with men who were real men according to what He says a man is. Manhood God's way required some practical changes. Through reading and studying the Bible God moved me to change my surroundings, to change the folks that I hung out with and invested time with. He even prompted me to change some of the places that I frequented. As I began to read and study the Bible, I got a clearer understanding of who God is. I began to comprehend the love that God has for me, and I got a clearer understanding of the purpose that God has for my life. I began to understand what Jesus did on the cross for me. I started to realize what the Bible says and how it directs and guides our lives.

This relationship with the Lord was all new to me, so I made a lot of missteps. I wasn't perfect. At times it was difficult, because I still had some of the old cravings and the things in me that had been passed down from my dad and his dad. The more I came to know God through His word and the more I recognized His personal love for me, the less these negative things had a pull on me. Through the reading of God's word my mind was being transformed. Romans 12:2 says "No longer be conformed to the pattern of this world, but be transformed by the renewing of your mind so that you might be able to test and discern God's good and perfect will for your life."

Again, the transformation was a process, one that I definitely had (and still continue) to go through. A lot of missteps, like I said, but it was a process that I was willing to take because I knew that there were things about me that needed to change. I had to be honest with myself. I had to face myself. As I began to go through this transformation it was like peeling back an onion. I started to see the different layers of stuff that I had accumulated in my life. God became my strength, and by His strength I was able to break old habits and develop new ones - good ones that pleased Him. As God moved people out of my life, He started moving men into my life that were beneficial to my walk with Him.

God took away the non-beneficial associations and moved men into my path who would help me walk the path that He had laid out for me.

Some of those old friendships changed gradually and others were immediate. God had to walk me through this process because it was somewhat painful. I couldn't do it alone in my own strength. These old friends were people I used to run with, but I had come to realize that they weren't part of the equation or part of God's plan for my life. They weren't on the same path that I chose to walk.

I remember expressing to some of my friends that I had decided to become a Christian and live out a Christian life. Some of them would say things like 'You just hit a bump in the road. You're going through a hard time in your life right now. Don't worry about it, you'll bounce back. Before you know it, you'll be back to the same old Craig.' But that's not what I wanted. I didn't like what I saw in my past, and I was determined not to turn back. I learned to use God as my measuring stick instead of society's standard or the opinion of others.

Now in terms of relating to God as my Father, it was tough because my experience with my earthly father had shaped my perception of a father. I was still carrying the baggage of distrust that my earthly father had handed me, which I inadvertently carried right into my relationship with God. I unconsciously held onto the mindset that one day my Heavenly Father might somehow disappoint me just like my earthly father had done. But as I read God's word and saw His faithfulness to the people that I was reading about, I began to see His faithfulness to me as well. I started to reflect on some of the things that I did and realized that they would have turned out differently were it not for the grace of God. I started to realize that God really does love me.

The more I read and studied Gods word, the more His word settled in my heart. The more His word settled in my heart, the more I began to know Him. The more I got to know Him, the more I trusted Him. The more I trusted Him, the more I love Him with the love that He first loves me with. And so began the cultivation of my relationship with God, which continues to this day.

Like the psalmist David said in Psalm 119:11, "I hide Your word in my heart that I might not sin against You." I love and trust God because I see that He's not a man that He can lie. God honors His word. So, I trust Him with my life. I love Him more and more. I'm ever more conscious of intentionally obeying Him, because all that He has in store for me is perfect for my life. He means me no harm. God has my best interest at heart.

I couldn't say the same thing about my dad. It was a long road, but I eventually came to the place where I was able to separate the two. My earthly reference point (my dad) was no longer my vantage point. I'm now able to see things through God's real and personal love for me.

In retrospect I see that God loved me all along. I didn't recognize it back then, but when I was a kid He gave me coaches that were good examples of manhood. (God works differently for each man.) I think God just set it up that every coach I played for was an ex-military guy. My coaches were disciplined men. Playing sports under such discipline gave me a level of respect for guys who were older than me, which in turn encouraged my desire to excel. Whether I was playing my first two loves, football or baseball, or playing basketball which came later down the road, I learned disciplined living from the examples displayed by my coaches. My coaches weren't sitting around reading the Bible with me. However, under their leadership there was a level of discipline instilled in me through sports that helped me in my process to becoming a man.

A lot of guys don't have the fortune of being taught discipline by older men. Consequently, for many the biggest challenge is understanding or relating to authority figures. In my opinion, a lot of men struggle with authority because the person who was supposed to be the authority figure in their lives didn't carry out his responsibility. The result is unfinished broken men walking around in society, unfinished because they were never taught how to deal with adversity and obstacles. They were never taught how to deal with Conflict, Controversy and Challenges (what I refer to as the 3 C's). As a result, we see the lack of guidance displayed through their frustrations and by the manner in which they respond to the 3 C's.

Like so many others, before I knew how to respond when faced with uncomfortable situations I'd react with frustration, anger and resentment. Over time the discipline of sportsmanship exhibited and taught by my coaches helped me to deal with the 3 C's in sports as well as in life. I learned how to channel my energy in a positive way in order to get positive results. As an athlete I learned that I had to put my own personal aspirations to the side for the good of the team if we were to defeat the opponent.

Today when I do prison ministry, I see young men who have gravitated to negative role models because they lacked positive ones. I come across young men who have multiple children that they cannot take care of. I see men who have not been taught what it means to be a man or what it means for a man to live up to his responsibilities. I see men who committed themselves to a gang or to friends when they were on the streets, but once incarcerated they don't so much as get a call from those who they've committed their lives to. For the most part they are forgotten by most everyone but their mother and grandmothers. I've met some men who have gotten caught up in the system and they spend the rest of their lives on a treadmill. They continue to relive the ills that they've been exposed to and they're stuck in the resentment and anger, which fuels their behavior.

On the other hand, I know of some men who live as free men in spite of the prison walls that confine them. These are men who have given Jesus Christ full reign to direct and use them as He sees fit. God's life-changing power is clearly evident in their lives, and they have more freedom than many who are out here walking the streets. They are living proof that a person can live a life of freedom, even behind bars.

To the contrary, you can be out here walking the streets, working, have a Ph.D., a Masters Degree or anything else, and be imprisoned trying to figure out life. The truth of the matter is, the man who does not have a relationship with Christ is a man who lives in a state of emotional and spiritual bondage, and he exists without the realization of true freedom. The man who seeks genuine change is a man who continues to cultivate a relationship with God through His Son Jesus Christ. The man who is truly free is the man who patterns his life after Jesus Christ. That man surrenders his will and his pain over to God and lets God relieve him of the baggage that he's been carrying throughout his life. That man is free to be a better man according to God's standard of manhood.

DEAR COUSIN DEBORAH,

Salutations, blessings and prosperity be unto you. I scribe to ask you with sincere humility; and if you can find it in your heart to bestow this favor, my gratitude you will always have.

I'm incarcerated and alone, and I'd appreciate it if you would post this missive where it can be broadly viewed.

I thank you and wish you well.

Silent and Solitary
Silent and solitary, I sit here alone
Surrounded by walls, cold steel and stone
Imprisoned by man, the punishment due
Struggling within, this time to go through.

Silent and solitary, captive honor is none
Tormented thoughts, the pain has begun
Fighting to live, yet living to die
Sanity tested, still wondering why.

Silent and solitary, I long to be free
Crying within, why is it me?
Love I once knew, stuck in the past
Wishful thinking travels the miles vast.

Silent and solitary, I must carry on
Awaiting the day when the hurt will be gone
Silent is best, my mind free to roam
Solitary until the day I go home.

Ronald R. Hines
Lebanon, OH

Protect him, Lord. You be his continued defense, so that he's never standing alone. Let him always be aware that he is empowered by You.

Toney Designz
ToneyDesignz@yahoo.com

BLACK MEN

E. Lavar Iverson

We are strength and struggle. We are stereotyped, oppressed, optimistic, and ignorant. We are violent, lost, and misguided. We are righteous, humble, troubled, gifted, and talented. We are separated. We are incarcerated.

The Struggle: From the beginning, like so many others, I was born into struggle. I was born E. Lavar Iverson at Kings County Hospital in Brooklyn, New York. I'm the youngest of eight siblings. Even though I had both of my parents, I grew up in a single parent household. My mother did her best to make the most out of what little we had. I saw my mother's struggle from as far back as I can remember, and it upset me. Yeah, my pops came through, but not often. This upset me. When he did come through, he was usually drunk. This upset me. As far as I can recall my parents were never together. Needless to say, this too upset me.

> *A financially unstable home, and a household void of a father to learn from makes life very difficult.*

Because of this I started to become violent, inattentive in school, misguided, troubled, and inevitably ignorant of life's big picture.

> *When a person's foundation is not uplifting and grounded in righteousness, he is easily enticed by the negative.*

Don't get me wrong, Mama-Love did a great job. She taught me and my siblings what she could. She did her best, but I still went contrary to her teaching.

Troubled: By the time junior high school came around, I wanted to explore the street life for the same reasons that our young Black brothers do today - fly clothes, fly cars, and fly women. Mama-Love did what she could to keep us fly. But I didn't have everything the other kids had, which upset me. So, I went to the streets to learn how to get what I wanted. This drive pulled me into small crime, boosting and selling weed so that I could have the latest fashions. Once I got educated in 'the field', the street hustle came easy for me. The next thing I knew I was going to school with drug money in one pocket and a gun in the other.

My mother saw my downward transition and was dead-set against it. In her quest to get help for me she contacted the authorities. She thought it would be a good idea for me to go to a group home. But that idea went out the window the day school security guards found a gun in my possession. Her baby, the youngest of her children, was a juvenile facing criminal charges.

I was sent to the Division of Juvenile Justice (DJJ) for 18 months. This hurt Mama-Love. Even though she wanted me off the streets for a while, 18 months was far longer than she'd expected or even wanted. I thought the same thing. So, from early 1994 to mid-1995 I was in DJJ custody doing the school and basketball thing. While there I was determined to better myself and to improve in the areas that I was lacking. I didn't know too much about self. Time away in DJJ helped, but then again it didn't.

The Gifted: I learned that I shared the same last name with this dude in college who was set to be the next M.J. (Michael Jordan), which made me do well in school and on the basketball court. You couldn't tell me that he wasn't my family member or that my skills weren't just like his. I took my DJJ team to the championships. But on game day I had a visit from my mother, sister, and nephews that kept me from playing. My team ended up losing the championship game by 4 points because I wasn't there.

I did 15 out of the 18 months because of good behavior. When I got out, I went to live with my pops in Crown Heights, Brooklyn. By then my mother was staying with one of my older sisters in her one-bedroom apartment that already had my two sisters and my nephew in it. It was crazy. This upset me. I stayed there with them a couple of nights until my pops had everything ready for me to stay with him. I didn't really want to live with him, but once there it was like I lived there by myself. My pops worked in a hospital and hung out. So, I only saw him when it was time to rest and on the weekends, his off days. My pops didn't really have rules like my moms. He basically let me do me at a young age. At that time I was only 16, and not ready for the responsibilities of a full-grown Black man. Without any house rules governing me, I was still driven by foolishness.

Misguided: Later I attended Wingate High School. I was promoted to the next grade because I did well in the DJJ School. But not long after I got home from DJJ I started slipping big time, for my own reasons; one of which was a name in the streets. I thought cutting school, selling drugs, and carrying weapons was cool. I later realized that this foolish activity was my downfall. These things led me to drop out of school in the 12th grade to sell drugs full-time (no good).

The Righteous: My message to the young Black men out there is please brothers, don't let this be you. Understand your gift early, your talent, and righteous living. If you don't, you might find yourself in a similar situation as me - incarcerated, serving 45 to life for a crime I didn't commit.

My running the streets brought on my present condition. Do you see how karma works? Even though I'm innocent of the crime for which I'm serving, I was no angel. I surrounded myself with negativity, and now look. I believe and see that this is a wake-up call for me, because I am wiser now, educated, righteous, talented, gifted, and humble. I am struggle and strength. I will get another chance at life.

Before any of my brothers out there make this mistake, I encourage you to do right from the gate. This will make your whole life straight. If no one is around to teach you righteousness or how to live upright, just learn from those of us who came before you. You don't have to make the same mistakes. Watch our wrong moves and purposely choose not to make them yourself. Read a lot of good information and books of substance and you'll begin to teach yourself. There's so much more that I would like to express to my brothers, but this is a collective message. Hopefully, my other Black brothers will convey what's needed to uplift our Black men.

There are real life stories, messages, as well as knowledge to be learned from the music of my words. So, until we link again Black man, stand up. It's our time.

Rest in peace to my sister and brother, Thedra Denise Iverson and Darrin Calvin Iverson.

BLACK MAN
in AMERIKKA

ANTWON E. M.

Where do I begin? How about I start with the man in the mirror…

I was born December 21, 1983 in St. Johns Hospital, Yonkers, New York. I was the first of seven. For some reason I don't have many memories of my younger years as a child. However, the one thing I do remember is never seeing my father. I don't know his laugh or his walk. In fact, I don't even know what he looks like. My mother spent much of her time in the streets and another portion of it in prison. As a result, I didn't have a firm foundation to stand on. Granted I had grandma, a few aunts and an uncle, but I still became a product of who my parents were. Does this story sound too familiar? It probably does. If it doesn't, you can probably relate to it in some way.

Dr. Martin Luther King, Jr. once said, "Men hate each other because they fear each other. They fear each other because they don't know each other. They don't know each other because they are separated from each other." Let's forget about race for a moment. We as a people worry about the wrong things. We focus on the things that divide us, rather than on the things that unite us, divisions like; I'm Guyanese, he's Sudanese, she's Puerto Rican, and the girl she walks past everyday on her way to work is Dominican. We really believe we are different. Our cultures may be different but we are the same people.

We use the notorious 'N' word as a term of endearment, and somehow we've found affection in leashing our women with a label that equates them to female dogs. We use derogatory words to describe ourselves without even knowing their origin. Surely this is ignorance. However, we always find ways to somehow justify our wrong with a right. We mistreat our women and abandon our children.

Who are we? We are Black men lost in America! All of us aren't this way, though. Much love to my brothers who know their way and their real worth. But what are a few compared to many? How will you ever believe you're a king, if you've grown accustomed to being the jester?

Harriet Tubman said it best, "I could have freed thousands more, if they had known they were slaves." Most of us have been down for so long we think it's where we belong.

Do you know who you are? Can you feel the pain of your ancestors? Do you even realize how important you are? Can you taste the blood of those before you?

The cries of my people echo deep
Within my soul
I can feel their fear each time the
White man is near
They laid in filth aboard slave ships
Fought to stay alive so we could live
Here we are, direct descendants of theirs
We are more valuable than we can imagine
So beautiful, yet we don't even know
Possess a light that won't even show
We live through them, as they through us
The very essence of who I am
Bears fruit from their tree of life…
Their knowledge.

Yes, I am a king, yet, I don't even show it
My sister, you are a Queen
And you don't even know it
We are alone ~ I don't even know where I am I've
lost touch with who I am
This foreign land I awoke in
Native tongue unspoken
My warrior spirit, broken

Will I ever realize who I am?
Will I ever grow?

Why must history repeat itself?
I know about the new Jim Crow
From my throne I have fallen
I can't remember my culture
I abuse my woman
Prey on my brother like a vulture
I feel the rage inside of me
The shame inside of me
Can you imagine what it's like
Hiding the pain inside of me?
I know what I must do
I know who I must be
Through knowledge of oneself,
I profess the king inside of me
A beauty I must define, a soul no longer on ice, A
Black man well refined.

I speak very little of my past, because where I come
from is frivolous compared to where I'm going. I
didn't bother to mention past failures, because who

I was doesn't stand a chance against who I am becoming.

CHANGE

RYAN ROBERTS

To be a Black man means (to me) that you have no other option but to commit to excellence. I believe that a life that is not committed to excellence is a life that is already behind the eight ball. The outcome of living contrary to a life of excellence is comparable to building a house on sand. We know that a house built on sand is not sturdy enough to withstand the storms that will inevitably come its way. At the end of the day, a life lived outside of the pursuit of excellence will not bear good fruit.

To bear good fruit and to positively impact lives you must have pure intentions. Furthermore, if you're spiritual and you believe in the Lord, then your intentions must be grounded in God's principles. God's principles will take you further than you could ever imagine.

Being a Black man in America is challenging. Black men encounter so many opposing forces. A Black man is all too often met with inaccurate stereotypes when he walks into an establishment. In order to move forward he has to stay focused on his objectives and step over the negative preconceptions. Real talk - he needs to step over the dumb stuff and focus on his reason for being. He must NEVER allow the negative stereotypes to dictate his outcome, decisions, or his drive. A forward-thinking man can and will use the negative stereotypes as a spring board to his success, even though he must put forth more of an effort than his colleagues. My insight - my experience.

As a business professional in the corporate arena I have achieved quite a bit of success working in very competitive roles at several Fortune 500 companies. Despite my successes, my accomplishments were discounted and considered 'less than' the work of my counterparts who achieved far less. I have had to perform and produce above and beyond my counterparts in order to begin to compete for advancement. It's only after having created a track record of excellence that I received a semblance of the comfortables that my colleagues were receiving all along.

Unlike myself, my colleagues don't have to overlook or maneuver around a load of negative stereotypes for people to feel at ease with them. A Black man in America often has to endure more than his counterparts. However, at the end of the day he can't put a price tag on the benefits received from his pursuit of excellence.

Hardship plus excellence builds perseverance, develops character and fortifies integrity, especially when you're committed to the ways of the Lord. It is God who gives the strength to stand

and withstand pressure. It is God who gives the courage to continue to do the right thing.

Many of us are not privy to the educational tools that exist in other communities. Even though this disadvantage has delayed many, our progress over the past decades is due in part to the resiliency of our people.

Despite having started off on an uneven playing field, I continue to succeed because of my commitment to excellence God's way. I continue to walk in faith with the knowledge that God will see me through. I'm committed to doing the right thing, whether people notice or not. Why? Because, the Lord is going to give me what's mine and give everyone else what's theirs. This is how I live and do business. Going through life this way means that I don't live with regret or with anything hanging over my head. We were not designed to live in defeat, guilt, regret, or in the shadow of anything lingering over our heads.

My initial decision to pursue excellence came the day I made a critical life changing decision. I came to a point in my life where I had to choose a side. I had to ask myself if I was going to accept God's way or was I going to accept what society tells me is ok. I chose God's way. Is God's way always easy? No. But He gives a level of satisfaction that you can't put a price tag on. Above all, God gives a level of peace that you just can't explain.

When life's challenges get heavy and things around you get crazy, you experience an overriding comfort when you live with the intent to walk in excellence and operate according to God's truth. Without this level of peace and security a young man is easily attracted to trouble that comes through peer pressure and gang affiliated friends. He's even susceptible to vice introduced by people he's exposed to on a regular. And of course, in the absence of a good role model like a good father, a young man can easily be lured into wrong living. Both parents need to be present, available and on guard for their sons as well as their daughters.

My father was absent from our family, so I didn't grow up in a conventional household. I knew who he was, but he had his own life. Do I love and care for him? Of course I do, but I didn't grow up with him.

Now my mother, she was a force in my life. She was in the Church. I grew up in the Pentecostal Church. I was one of those kids who used to dance up and down the aisles. I was also a latch-key kid. I walked to and from school alone as early as age 5 or 6. By age 6 or 7 I was preparing my own dinners. By the time I was 8 I'd walk up the street alone to do my laundry at the laundromat. Around age 9 I moved in with my grandparents, and then with my aunt and uncle who ended up being very lax. As early as 13, I'd find myself outside at 3 in the morning just chilling and breaking night. My mother was around, but her influence had faded a bit by then. By age 13 I'd already been working a year, which led to my increased independence. As a result of my assumed independence my mother and I clashed during my teenage years. In spite of whatever obstacles I may have had, I accepted my independence and made the most of life. That all mushroomed on me one day and I came to the realization that my life needed a drastic change.

I was an adult by then. I had a girlfriend, but that wasn't working out. So, one day I found myself alone in the house. During that time I'd spend days without speaking to anyone. Then one day as I sat home in painful silence, it hit me like a ton of bricks. "I'm all alone. I don't have anyone in my life." That realization struck and I became overwhelmed with emotion. Then I heard an audible voice that told me to go to the window and say a couple of words. I did just that. I kid you not, it was like a movie. About thirty or so birds came out of nowhere, sat on the branches of the tree outside the window, and started chirping unusually loud. Then I heard a voice as clear as day say, "You're not alone." At that point I almost lost it. I couldn't believe it. I called up my mother to tell her. When I mentioned that experience to a few other people, I felt like nobody really believed me.

Another night shortly after that, I was in a park alone waiting for my girlfriend. It had just finished raining and an unusually heavy fog had settled in the area. I could barely see through the opaque fog. As I sat thinking about my life I got overwhelmed and started to tear up. Then like the time before, an audible voice said to me, "Say a couple of words." As I was about to speak a few words, in an instant out of nowhere I felt something rise from the bottom of my feet to the top of my head. I opened my eyes and the fog was completely gone. The sky was clear, the moon and stars were bright and in clear sight. At that point I made my life changing decision to walk with Christ. That's when my whole life began to change for the good.

I can say that my decision to choose Christ as head of my life was my defining moment. God changed me. He changed my life. If I tell anyone else about life, I can only tell them from this perspective. God is real. I can attest to that. I can tell people that God does hear our prayers, and He's here to help.

Over time I started to see my desires come to fruition. My goal to be an entrepreneur was realized when I launched my first business. That business eventually mushroomed into other businesses. God changed my direction, and my life finally began to get on track for the good.

If you want to change your direction and get on track, ask God to take over. He'll step in and redirect your life. God will draw you closer to Him, and you will experience Him in a new and real way. The change process isn't easy because it counters mainstream thought. Contrary to popular opinion, commit to honesty in the face of a culture that endorses stretching the truth, lies (spin), determine to show love and compassion to someone who might have given you a dirty word or rubbed you the wrong way. When God changes you, He gives you what you need to swim against popular belief and public pressure. He gives you victories in ways you never could have achieved on your own.

A man who wants change must eventually arrive at the place where he defines what is important to him. He must determine whether or not going in a positive direction is more important than going in a negative one, and whether or not being kind and compassionate is more important than being sneaky and rude. It's a personal decision that only he can make.

I talk about my experiences knowing full well that every man lives and sees through his own experiences, and each man will run his own course. I speak with encouragement to say that there's a better way to run this course called life. That better way will give comfort and peace of mind. It will give a level of understanding that just can't be obtained any other way.

Another thing, when all else fails (and even before that) just talk to God. Pray and He will show up. Believe me, He shows up in subtle ways that you wouldn't even think. He'll show up every day. The more you get to know Him, the more you see the ways in which He will show up. Real talk - relationship brings revelation.

I have to say that the change that I needed in order to walk on top of the stereotypes and over every other negative element really didn't happen until my back hit the wall and I committed my life to the Lord. That's when I saw the significant change in me. That's when I began to strive for excellence God's way.

UN-CYCLED

LeMar Connor

I am presently an incarcerated young Black man in America. I share with you an abridged version of my life so that you can begin to understand my plight and who I am as a Black man in America.

I was born in the early 80's. Not long after my 2nd or 3rd birthday my father abandoned me and my mother, leaving me to be raised solely by my mother, other family members, and by whichever man that came into our lives. When I was a toddler my mother met and fell in love with my godfather who became an influential father figure in my life. He raised and loved me as if I were his own son.

He instilled in me morals, values, and principles. He taught me about respect and honesty. He also introduced me to many interests, activities, and cultures beyond those in our Bronx neighborhood. Over time I grew very fond of him. I developed a deep admiration and respect for him. This man was and did for me what my own father wasn't and didn't.

Even though my father was absent from my life and I had a new father figure, I started to see how much my father and I were alike. I was headstrong and increasingly angry. The anger that I harbored turned into resentment that festered into hatred for my father. I had grown tired of the lies and broken promises. My dear mother, who was employed as a police officer, was also tired. She was tired of having to explain my father's broken promises each time he failed to visit me as he said he would. The combination of my anger, stubbornness, and resentment was the source of my rebellion towards my mother and godfather. I grew so rebellious that I'd lie to them and steal money from them to buy the things that I felt I needed. I was one of the smartest students in my class and was generally a good kid, but my anger caused me to make irrational decisions.

By the age of 12 I was already sexually active. I learned about sex from watching pornography. I started smoking weed at age 13 and was selling it at 14. All the while I was packing bags at the local supermarket to buy my own Jordans and outfits. Shortly after that, late in the summer of '93 I became a member of a gang. Within that same year a classmate introduced me to the business of selling crack cocaine.

My very first night in the business I worked about 4 ½ hours selling crack to people from all walks of life. Some of my customers were homeless people. Some were regular folks. But most were 9-5 working and upper-class white people in furs walking poodles or wearing suits and carrying briefcases. The crack moved quickly. That night I made $1,200 for myself. It was the night that changed my life and threw me deeper into the revolving cycle of death that so many Black men in America get sucked into today.

During that same time my mom and godfather split up, for which I was partly to blame. My mother started working over-time. While she was working and doing double shifts to maintain household expenses, her only son was knee deep in the drug game, gang life, and having sex with multiple females, some twice my age. Drawn by the addiction for fast money, women, power, and clothes that selling crack gave me, I fell deeper into the abyss of the street life. I didn't find out until late in the game that prison and or death were a possibility. I was blinded by my lust and infatuation for the materialistic gain that drug dealing provided.

No one schooled me on how to be a drug dealer. I learned the ins and outs of drug dealing on my own through trial and error. There were opportunities for me to be schooled on the greater and better things in life, perhaps by an older male family member, and not just by my absentee father. I could have listened to and learned from a male figure, not just because of the relationship or my admiration for him, but because of his example of manhood. I realize that it takes a man to raise a man. No disrespect or offense, but truth is truth. A man can't teach a female how to be a woman, and a female can't teach a male to be a man any more than a rose can produce a tulip.

Much praise and respect is due to my mother who raised and cared for me to the best of her ability. I as a man take full responsibility for my actions, because this is what a man does. However, I do know that if my father, who I now love and respect, had been a man and taken responsibility for me when I was a child as he was supposed to, maybe just maybe things would have turned out different for me. I was my father's responsibility. He was supposed to raise me to the best of his ability and teach me right from wrong, instead of leaving me to learn on my own, through friends, or from the street. For every action there's an equal or greater reaction. If my father had only done his part, I think it would have changed the turn of events that led to my incarceration.

I've been incarcerated for the past ten years. I'm no longer the person caught up in the middle of everything. I am now the person who has grown wise through knowledge and experience. Like Malcolm X, I have turned prison into my university. I take my present situation and make the best of it. My incarceration has made me a stronger and better person overall. I'm determined to break the chain and cycle of the older generations that failed to give proper guidance and education to the younger generations. This cycle will cease once I have my own child. I know firsthand the effects and damage caused by the lack of communication between generations; whether the communication lapse be between father and son, uncle and nephew, or any other senior to junior relationship.

I remember as a child envying my cousins for having both parents in the house. I even envied the fact that my cousins had siblings to grow up with. I wanted a father and sibling in the house so much that I hung out with my cousins to fill the void that I felt. I even grew angry at my mother for not having another child. I felt so alone.

Once during a family party in a Harlem park two of my cousins teased me for not having a father in my life. Their taunting cut me to the heart and made me angry. I ended up going alone to a different part of the park. I either broke a bottle or picked up a piece of broken glass. I confronted them with tears in my eyes and broken glass held tightly in my hand. I wanted them to physically feel the pain that I felt in my heart. If not them, then I wanted to hurt myself. But they ran.

I was always pretty smart. I was one of the smartest in my class, but I had also become the class clown. My behavior frequently landed me in the school psychiatrist's office. During my visits to the school psychiatrist I'd openly place the blame for my disruptive behavior on the fact that I lacked a father. Nothing changed. Instead, things got worse. My father's absence became the gateway that led to a corridor of other problems as I got older.

The plight of the Black man in America today is not one that we created for ourselves. It is one we subconsciously and consciously continue to practice and perpetuate by our thoughts and actions. Black man, if we change our thinking, we can change our reality. We must become enlightened by truth and the knowledge of who we are. We must know our purpose for being here on earth. Once we do these things, we can change our actions from the negative to the positive, which will then change our plight, not only in America but in the world.

Black men, (people as a whole), need to unite for the good. United, we are a force to reckon with. If Black people worldwide would unite, we would do exponentially more good than an atomic bomb can do damage. We should not be our own worst enemy, destroying ourselves like rivals in a civil war. If we come together for the good, we can eradicate the wrongs that affect our society.

WAR

BROTHER REGINALD

This is not life as it's supposed to be! This is life in its worst form. America the land of the free? Or is this a scene from the Bible - a war against good and evil?

My story isn't really important. I was born in St. Luke's Women's Hospital, July 3, 1987 to a beautiful mother. My father turned his back on me from the moment of my birth. I'm not the first, nor will I be the last. As early as I can remember, all I really knew was being cared for by the women in my family. My mother isn't the richest woman financially, but she's the wealthiest in spirit. She's a strong, focused, courageous and trustworthy individual. I could go on for years about her and the strong women in my life. I really want to share a message to the blind Black man in America in hopes of raising that 'fold and giving light.

My father is who I want to focus on: From the day I was born he made it very clear that he didn't want me. We never spent a Christmas, Thanksgiving, Easter, or let alone my birthday together. Sadly, as a man today, I can't say that I blame him for his absence. He did to me what was done to him, and to his father, and to many of my ancestors. Call it the 'Willy Lynch Stratagem'. It's the doctrine of creating and keeping a nigger.

This savage-man, William Lynch, purportedly spread the poisonous formula for the handicapping, destruction, and manipulation of the Black man. It's been said that he was so sure of his method that he guaranteed that if followed, slave owners would be able to control the Black man for centuries. Think about it. How long has it been to date?

Since the beginning of Black men in the Americas we Black men were taught to hate one another, whether it be for skin complexion, age, height, size or whatever. We've become enslaved to the falsity that the only thing that's right is white, to the extent that we spend hundreds of millions on 'things' in order to have the similitude of whiteness. We foolishly pay for an image while we still live in substandard tenement housing, and some of us are even dying in the process.

A tactic used years ago to strip Black men of their manhood was to take the strong Brother, tie his limbs to two opposite facing horses and set the horses' tails on fire. The horses would run in opposite directions to escape the fire, and the man would be split in two as his family and other Black men looked on. This was done to break the man - the foundation of the family. So you see, how can I blame my father for upholding what was instilled and reinforced in him before he was born? My father was misled and was never able to break the weights that had him shackled.

> *As time progressed so many of us Black men fell victim to the streets in search of a place of belonging.*

We were enslaved on plantations. We were forced to work the land or perform some other backbreaking inhumane work. Then, when the Black man needed to purchase any kind of item for daily living, he had to shop at the plantation store with the 10 or 20 cents earned from slave labor and sharecropping for the week. He basically worked for free, which is the same thing we're doing right now either behind these prison walls or at home on those broken streets.

Now I ask you brothers to look back at what I've said and tell me whether I lied about any of it. I think it is time we as Black people unite and create for ourselves. No nation will ever respect us or take us seriously if we can't unite amongst ourselves. How can we be loyal to anything or anyone else, if we're not first loyal to ourselves?

Your brother in the struggle, Brother Reginald

CHOICE

ALVA WILLIAMS, JR.

Back when I was in high school, I had a serious football injury that landed me in the hospital for almost a year. The injury eventually cost me my leg. At the beginning of my hospital stay I laid in the intensive care unit a few feet from a gentleman whose body was just an upper torso. From a little below the waist down there was nothing. He too was there as a result of an accident. The difference between the two of us was that he was smiling and I was not. I couldn't figure out what he had to smile about. He had very little life left. And, what could he do even if he did live? I couldn't understand it. He was just half of a body, but he was smiling. And there I was in a slump with my lower torso intact, despite my severely injured leg.

I felt like I had a lot more to smile about than he did. Yet he was smiling and I wasn't. What could he possibly have to smile about? It was just illogical to me. I kept studying him. The more I watched him my rationale for being in a slump grew increasingly more illogical.

The guy and I never spoke. He was dead by morning. The fact that he had been smiling made the difference to me because it was out of the norm. As far as I could see there was absolutely no reason for his smile. The truth of the matter is that most people with far less injury would not have been smiling. His unusual disposition and my quest for an answer became the catalyst for my growth.

During my search I purposely read about the Apostle Paul in the Bible. I read how he was shipwrecked, stranded and imprisoned. In spite of it all he was content and full of joy. I'd often ponder how it was that Paul could maintain his contentment and joy under such bleak circumstances. He was locked up, mistreated and even beaten. Then I saw it. Paul was looking at life through a totally different lens, and that's why he could sit back and withstand the hardship…with a smile.

I knew something was there and I finally realized that Paul had something. I just needed to know what. I eventually found the 'what'. It's viewpoint. Both the Apostle Paul and the dying man in that hospital had a totally different viewpoint from the average person. It was then that I realized that my perspective had to change in order for me to grow as a man. The lens through which I viewed life needed a definite change. Up until that point I knew that something was off balance in my life, but I didn't know what it was or why it was off balance. On top of that, I didn't know what 'in balance' looked like.

As God would have it, I was introduced to a group of men who behaved totally different from the 'average' male. What I saw in them differed from what I'd seen elsewhere. These men stood out, away from, and in front of the crowd. Their mannerisms were different. How they spoke to each other was different. How they interacted with their wives was different. As odd as it was, it felt normal to me. And I wanted 'it', whatever 'it' was. The lens that I saw through prior to this new revelation needed changing. I could no longer hold onto the viewpoint of the masses if I wanted to grow. And so, I made the conscious decision to see, think, and behave differently.

Like everyone else I see through lenses that have been tinted by life experiences, by my upbringing, and by the world around me. It's as if we've been strapped with a pair of lenses that cloud our vision. But then as the lenses are cleaned we begin to see with increased clarity.

Here's a simplistic view of how I see it: It's sort of like what happens as we read the Bible. We read the Bible and our experiential viewpoint at that particular point in time filters out what we're able to absorb. As the filters are removed, what we read becomes more apparent to us. The revealed message isn't new. It's always been there. We simply receive new revelation as the filters are removed. The clarity of the message then evokes change.

Of course, the clearing of vision is a process. Change started for me the day I decided that I no longer wanted to be on this ride called life with my eyes clouded. I chose to see, and in so doing God removed and continues to remove the filters. Here's an example of how it works for me: On one day I might not have clear understanding of something I've read in the Bible. On another reading I grasp the message. And yet, on another reading of that same scripture the message revealed is different but congruent to the previous revelation. Each new revelation is exactly what I need at that precise point in my personal development. The process is ongoing, and that's growth.

Now as far as the transformation specific to my manhood, it cannot be classified according to race because manhood is manhood regardless of racial identity, creed or religion. I was born a male, but I made the conscious decision to be a man according to God's specific design. Yes, I believe manhood is a choice. Contrary to popular opinion, simply being born with a Y chromosome and all of the accompanying parts no more makes a man than being strapped with a fully equipped tool belt makes a construction worker. The physical anatomy is but the obvious distinction between male and female. It is not the defining mark of manhood. Manhood is what manly life choices mature a male into. There's even a clear distinction between a boy and a man. That too extends beyond the existence and development of the physical anatomy.

Manhood for me was a deliberate transition from boyhood. I didn't just wake up one day to realize that I'd become a man. I made the conscious decision to be a man according to God's design, and then God led the way. As He leads, I continue to choose His way of living.

> *I am the compilation of my thoughts and the sum of my choices.*

Do I choose to behave like everyone else out in the street, or do I choose to be different? Do I choose to stay in bed, or do I get out of bed so I can productively face life and handle my responsibilities? Do I choose to read nudie magazines, or do I choose to read something beneficial? Do I choose to eyeball that woman as she walks past, or do I control my eyes and the thoughts that ensue? Do I choose to do right, or do I choose to do wrong? Deuteronomy 30:15 says "See, I [God] have set before you today life and good, death and evil…" The choice is mine.

Of course, I've made a boat load of bad choices throughout my life. In retrospect I see God's intervention and I see that He rescued me from what could have happened to me as a result of those decisions. I didn't try to figure this life thing out on my own. I simply made the choice to live life the best way, which is God's way. When I made that life-changing decision, God gave me the desire to live a right and fruitful life. He then opened doors to make things happen for me. The initial choice was for me to surrender and tell God that I was going to live life his way. I could not clean myself up or make myself perfect first. If I could, I wouldn't need God. I simply made the right choice, and God commenced to working on me according to His promise in Psalm 138:8, "God will perfect that which concerns me."

I equate the process of choice to grocery shopping. As with food shopping, we have before us an array of items to choose from, and we do so according to our desires and what best suits our needs. Well, in life God helps me to pick the right and necessary things that would add value and produce personal growth.

My dad walked through the same 'life-supermarket', but his choices were detrimental. What and how he made his selections didn't affect how I thought about him. I had to look past the detractors that he selected, simply because of my love for him. Everybody makes mistakes, so I couldn't get hung up on his. I chose to look past his shortfall in order to move forward into manhood according to God's specific plan for my life. However, I cannot take credit for my good choices. It is definitely God who leads me to make the best possible decisions.

Manhood can be daunting at times. It's a fight, but men are inherently fighters. There's something about rising to meet challenges and tackling responsibilities that gets my adrenalin pumping. The challenges of manhood are especially exciting once a man knows his value and position in relationship to God. For example, if I lived in a kingdom nation where my dad was king, as the son of the king my viewpoint, actions, and interactions would be from the perspective of my relationship to the king – I am the king's son. As a Christian this is my reality. My Heavenly Father is the King, and as His son I've been bestowed with an advantage that preceded my existence. When I see life from this viewpoint, I have every reason to smile, no matter the challenge.

> *When I know my value and the source of my strength, then I know that I've already conquered the challenges even before I step up to them.*

I sum it up like this: If you entered a football game against the toughest opponent and you knew before kickoff that you were going to win the game, you would play with an extraordinary confidence. Well, we have that confidence through Christ, which is what Apostle Paul saw. He experienced turbulence and pain that comes from just living, but he saw the reward that was revealed to him through Scripture and through his moment-by-moment relationship with Christ.

My closest associates are men who live out the realities of genuine manhood. They are men who know their true worth. I try to hang around these men every opportunity I get, because that's how I grow. The Bible says that iron sharpens iron. So, when I see some iron out there, I gravitate to it.

Despite the challenges, being in the hunt amidst other iron sharpeners makes life exciting. Today I smile because I know that the game is in my favor. I'm the winner before kickoff. When faced with tests and life's challenges, I can smile with the confidence that I already have the answers to the test, while so many others are sweating unnecessarily to just to pass.

To be a man you simply need to ask God to show you. God will open your eyes to the information that He has already placed around you. God will lead you to men who can show you what real manhood is according to His benchmark. From the onset to the close of the day, God's definition is

THE definition, and He doesn't care what you or I think about it. Manhood is what God says it is.

I don't have a seminary degree or a bunch of initials behind my name, but my prayer throughout the years is "Lord please give me wisdom. Please teach me." As an answer to prayer God pointed me to His word, the Bible. In spite of the strong dislike that I had for reading I read it anyway.

> *The blueprint for manhood is available to me and to any other male who wants it, but the choice to be receptive to it is all up to the individual.*

When I was a teenager the youth pastor encouraged me to "Read the Bible anyway, it'll eventually click." With each book and text read, I grew from the person who disliked reading to the person with an insatiable appetite for a productive word and good books. I've become fascinated with the Bible, so much so that every time I read God's word, I get a new revelation. With each read I'm confident that God is speaking to me and shaping me into the man according to His purpose.

The blueprint for manhood is available to any male who chooses to receive it. Likewise, the gift of salvation is free and available to any and all who will accept it. The choice is ours to take it or leave it.

We are surrounded by opportunities to allow God to teach, refine and clear our vision. Whether or not we choose to see the choices is up to us. And yes, the act of seeing is a choice. In order to see we need only to ask God to open our eyes.

> *Get around men who are handling their business. Right living is contagious.*

I thank God that He has placed me around men who exemplify authentic manhood, men who shoulder the responsibilities of being men. They don't avoid it like bachelors breaking their necks to dodge the garter at a wedding reception. I'm fortunate to be surrounded by men who line up under God's authority, men who look to God for direction so they can successfully lead those under their authority, men who love their wives and children. These men have made the conscious decision to do something that the average person wouldn't do, and that's to step away from the masses in pursuit of purpose.

By the way, what's up with bachelors running from the garter? I went to a wedding once where when the garter was tossed the bachelors scattered as if a grenade had been thrown into the crowd. The only one left standing was a three-year-old boy who caught the garter by default.

If you look at a household where the male is actually a man, that image might seem foreign because it differs from the household depicted by mainstream media. The media all too often portrays the man head of household as unnecessarily feminine, weak in character, or a psychotic abuser. Why? They don't have a clue what authentic manhood looks like. Shamefully, too many males have caught that same distorted viewpoint from the masses and from mainstream media. I'm mindful to get my viewpoint straight from the Source of manhood and not from the masses.

> *I operate with the mindset that if the herd is moving in one direction then I'll move in the opposite, because the herd is likely to be slaughtered.*

No person has the absolute formula for manhood. However, my advice to the man who has grown cold and is on the verge of shirking responsibility, get around men who are handling their business. Right living is contagious. You will catch on to it once you drop your defenses. It's like returning a piece of coal to the fire. The coal cools off when it is removed from the fire and heats back up once it is returned to the hot embers.

If a man is not doing what he was designed to do, everything under his authority and care suffers. His wife and his children will feel the undue weight of his mishandled responsibilities. If you find yourself slipping and cooling down, get around men who are standing strong on solid ground. Surround yourself with men who are on fire for the right things.

The road we travel is as individual and unique as one man's fingerprints to the other. The one thing we all have in common is the choice to be or not to be a man according to God's design. You need only to choose to walk God's path to manhood, and God will show you how to walk and where to step as you walk. He will place men around you to help guide you along the way. Make the choice, and God will clear your vision and change your viewpoint. Start where you are and let God run the ball.

If you're willing to make the change to manhood but you don't know how that change is going to happen, just make the commitment to change and let God take care of the process. The process is God's business anyway, not ours. We make the choice, and God uses everything in His arsenal to make the change in us. We open the door for that to happen by simply choosing God's way. The ball is in our court.

Manhood… It's a choice.

SHIFT

TYLIK WILLIAMS (VARLET ROSE)

I once saw a movie by the name of New Legend of Shaolin, starring the actor Jet Li. In the movie the character played by Jet Li gave his little child the choice between life and death by placing a toy and a sword in front of the child. The child was faced with the decision to choose one or the other. If the child chose the toy, he was sure to die. If he chose the sword, he would have inevitably chosen life, and a successful one.

Comparatively, the Black man in America has chosen the toy, that toy being the all too common façade of fly-ness: clothes, language, and actions. So many Black men in America have preferred to settle for this empty front that equates to death. The sword that so many fail to choose represents responsibility, discipline, sacrifice, and constructive struggle; the combination of which is the foundation of a life lived successfully. The average Black man in America shifts his weight to choose the toy. From who? His mother.

Let's take a look back to the time when African slavery in America was the way of the day. The enslaved mother would do everything in her power to prove her son incompetent, to keep the slave master from taking her son away. This was the beginning of a post-traumatic syndrome that subconsciously still exists in uneducated and miseducated Black mothers. Today you have mothers who hold their sons back by allowing them to be mis-labeled as 'special ed' by the MIS-education system, just so she can get a government check.

Here's a test: Go to the average disenfranchised home and hold up a picture of one of their own male children and say something like; *Oh, he's such a beautiful young man.* Don't be surprised if you hear, *Yeah, but he's bad, hard headed and just like his daddy.* How bad or hard-headed can a child actually be if he's being properly groomed? Maybe it's the parent(s) who's the bad one. Maybe it's the parent(s) who's delinquent in grooming their son for manhood. You can't tell me that a child has more power than his parent(s) to the point that he's out of control. This is the reality. Let's deal with it.

Another example: Let's say there's a household with five children, four of them being boys. Let's name one of the boys Deshawn, but everyone calls him Doc-Doc. Unfortunately, Doc-Doc is mentally challenged and because of it he receives the most attention from his parents. No matter how he looks, wears his clothes, speaks or acts, he is viewed by most as 'the baby'. The rest of the children wish to receive the same attention as Doc-Doc, so they imitate Doc-Doc's behavior transforming it into a form of coolness. From the retarded words spoken out of their mouths to the crippled walk that they tend to perform for others, this sense of being cool has become a debilitating epidemic amongst Black men in America. Coupled with buffoonery, this out of control epidemic has poured into the mainstream where mainstream now promotes and praises prison, gangs, violence, homosexuality and misogynist ways. This unnatural way of life has become a norm in Black America, ultimately affecting the Black man who has the duty to secure the foundation of the family.

The time is now to start shifting our babies towards the sword. Too much sport and play is never good. It's time to choose life. It's time to deal with the epidemic.

Ephesians 6:17
And take the sword of the Spirit, which is the word of God.

Toney Designz
ToneyDesignz@yahoo.com

FOUNDATION

JAMES BAZEMORE

Foundation: The solid place of support on which one stands, from which one is successfully launched

A much-needed place…

As far back as I can remember (between the ages of 3 and 5), family gatherings in my home most often resulted in everybody passed out (literally) from drinking, partying, etc. During those times my curiosity-filled mind naturally led me to the cigarette butts and leftover alcohol that remained in the glasses and styrofoam cups.

Fast forward to age 10: While growing up in Harlem's St. Nicholas Houses (the Projects), my family wasn't as fortunate as others. I was the youngest of four siblings raised in a single parent household. A direct consequence of not having a strong alpha male figure was that there was no direction, even though my Earth-Queen (Mother) tried her best as a woman. During those times my Pops was away incarcerated. I knew of his existence. My Earth-Queen had boyfriends, but we had very little if any guidance regardless of what level of chastisement or punishment was administered. After a while, the absence of a strong alpha male coupled with not having the latest fashions like my peers, I became what I now know as angry and resentful.

I experienced various stages of anger and resentment, which led to my acting out in school, fighting; and in one incident stabbing my neighbor in the eye with a pencil, which ultimately resulted in me being kicked out of NYC Public Schools.

My only alternative was placement at a 600 School, a school for youth deemed to be socially maladjusted and or emotionally disturbed. It was a place full of boys and armed security guards on post at the doors.

Within 2 to 3 years I began running away with a few locals from the projects where I lived. Around that same time in 1986, at the tender age of 12, I was formerly introduced to the 'Deuce', better known as 42nd Street Times Square, Midtown Manhattan. From the moment I was introduced, or better said exposed to the tall skyscrapers, bright lights, fast movement, and traffic, both legal and illegal, I was captivated by it all. Disney and the like have since taken over, but the same nefarious traffic coexists with the family-friendly entertainment today. It literally is the city that never sleeps.

I embraced the street life along with all it had to offer; the lying, stealing, cheating, robbing, deceiving, and homelessness. It all became the blueprint and foundation for my house built on quicksand. The events that transpired while I roamed blindly in a senseless pack that was led by the blind is what led me to a rather lengthy career of bouncing from juvenile institutions to group homes to foster homes, which eventually set the stage for my lengthy stay on Rikers Island.

I was convicted of a crime and sentenced to four years, and later released with no solid foundation to stand on. A couple of years later I was sentenced again for another felony. After serving my sentence, released again with no solid foundation. Not long after that release I was tried and convicted once again for another felony. This time I was sentenced as a career criminal, discretionary-persistent 3-time felon, facing 17 to life.

Though it's unfortunate, I'm a firm believer that any and all events transpire within the universe for a reason and purpose. I'm ashamed that I've spent the majority of my youth behind these walls.

However, I can honestly say that I now move with a good purpose while laying a strong foundation. I now surround myself with purpose driven like-minded individuals who also hold fast to the creed of having a firm foundation in this shaky world, and to the motto 'losing is not an option'.

A FATHER'S LOVE

PETER LAWSON

I am a son, a brother, a father, an uncle, a neighbor and a friend who holds relationships in high regard. Of the relationships dearest to my heart, my relationship with God is number one, followed by my relationship with my two children. In my early years of parenting I had my order of relationships out of place. I didn't know any better, so my children were first and God was second. Once I came into a relationship with Jesus Christ and made Him head of my life, I realized that I needed God as my priority in order to be a good father to my children. Over time I learned that

God, who is my Heavenly Father, is the perfect example of fatherhood.

I grew up in Jamaica, West Indies. We had a loving home, but it was not the typical family environment. My mother died when I was quite young and my father's job kept him away months at a time, as he worked throughout the Caribbean. For the most part I was raised by my older siblings after my mother's death. My father loved me, and I loved him. However, it was my ever-present Heavenly Father who showed me the truest depths of a father's love. I only wish to love and lead my children by the example that He continues to give me each day.

My bond with my Heavenly Father was established and set in motion when I was a relatively young Christian. I'd spend hours with the Lord each day. That period in my life was the beginning of my day-to-day, minute-by-minute conversational relationship with the Lord. Our times together and conversations were and still are a significant part of my life. I don't necessarily feel the need for long daily prayers, because I talk and listen to God throughout the day. When I worked in Manhattan, I'd often walk down the street talking to God as I intentionally wore earplugs so I could talk without people thinking I was crazy. There were other times when I'd spend my lunch hours talking with the Lord as I sat in the church across the street from my office. Those years were precious.

Me and God, we have a conversational type of relationship. Our conversations have become an integral part of who I am. God is my intimate friend with whom I can talk about anything. I look forward to spending time with Him, and I especially look forward to conversing with Him about my children.

My son and daughter are also an integral part of who I am. I enjoyed them as they were growing up and I enjoy them even more now that they are adults. I don't think a day passes without me praying for them. I look forward to our times together just as I did when they were children. I hang out with my son like buddies and take my daughter on dates. I watch movies with my kids, go out to dinner, and travel with them. We even sit and shoot the breeze.

I'm a firm believer that a father's relationship with his children is vital to their total wellbeing. I also believe that a dad is the first important man in a daughter's life. So, I open doors for my daughter, pull her chair out so she can sit, and I make sure that she's safe. As her father I'm setting the standard for any man who decides to court her. I want to be sure that she knows what to expect and that she knows not to settle for less. My daughter knows in her heart of hearts that I have her best interest in mind.

The most significant moment in my life as a father was when I started this walk of faith. I became a Christian and got scared to death that I'd mess up and that I wouldn't measure up as a father. That's when the Lord stopped me and told me not to worry. He told me to just treat my children the way He treats me. God had established the parameters for what I needed to do as a father. He created the blueprint for how I'm to treat my children. I became mindful of how my Heavenly Father treated me as I interacted with my children. Did I always get it right? Absolutely not! I'd mess up sometimes. There was one thing for sure, and that was that God didn't mess up with me.

Once when my son was younger, he said, "Dad when I grow up, I'm going to be just like you." If I didn't know the Lord my chest would have puffed up, but I knew my shortcomings and the grave responsibility that I had to live up to. My son's aspiration to walk in my footsteps was a bit overwhelming for me. I told him, "I don't want you to be like me. I want you to be like the One who I want to be like. I want you to be like God."

God has taught me a tremendous amount about fatherhood. He's even used my children's life lessons to teach me about life. I'm reminded of a time when my daughter was a little girl. She had a knack for knocking things over back then. One day as she sat at the dining table, she knocked over her cup of milk. I used to get really upset at things like that. She looked up at me, afraid that I was going to yell or get upset at her. I saw the fear in her eyes and realized how much I loved her. I just couldn't get angry. Instead, I knocked my drink over too. She just looked at me and asked, "Dad, you did that for me?" I know that was God's doing, even though I didn't know Him personally at the time.

My son, he was hyper. He was an over stimulated smart child that had been diagnosed and medicated for ADHD. At the same time, he was the kind of child that would read everything he could get his hands on. In his early years of elementary school, he had a teacher who saw in him what none of his previous teachers could see. This particular teacher saw an intelligent child with great potential. She saw my son and started asking him questions. She then asked the class if they knew what the barter system was, and my son proceeded to give her the correct answer. He knew the answer because I spent time teaching him and his sister about money and the history of monetary systems. The teacher was impressed by his intellect. She then realized that he was an excellent reader. My son ended up getting skipped to the next grade. In addition, the regular psychiatrist visits that he and his sister had ended as well. It was all done by God through prayer.

I prayed continuously for my children. Prayer changed my hyperactive lumbering son into a big gentleman. He's so gentle now that I'm amazed. I used to come home, and the boy would run and tackle me. He's been known to hug me and break my glasses. How could I get angry with someone who hugged me so passionately? I just couldn't. I could have snuck in the back door to avoid bruises, but my daughter would welcome me at the front door with her gentle hugs, and I didn't want to miss out on those. I miss those precious moments with them.

After my wife and I divorced our children lived with their mother. Despite the broken marriage, I was determined not to give fatherhood up in pursuit of other things or relationships. Regardless of the separation, my children knew that I was with them. They also knew that they could be with me anytime wherever I went. My son and daughter meant too much to me for me to take fatherhood lightly. Because they were and still are an integral part of my life, I'm mindful to look to my Heavenly Father for His help with fathering them. To this day I spend much time conversing with the Lord about them.

When my son was a teenager, he and I experienced a sequence of events that turned into a series of lessons for the both of us. It all started when my son walked through the train from one subway car to the next. When he got to the next subway car about five Transit Police Officers surrounded him. They pounced on him with a tirade of questions insinuating that he had some sort of criminal record, which he didn't and still doesn't. My son pacified the situation. However, to justify their harassment the officers gave him a $50 summons for walking through the train. The first chance he got he called me. Needless to say, I was angry. I told him not to worry because the problem was now mine and I was going to take care of it. Later when the police called to give him his hearing date, he handed me the phone. After I questioned the officer, I had a heart to heart conversation with my son. I talked to him about stereotyping and that he cannot expect people to judge his heart. He needs to do his best to present himself as a precaution to harmful stereotypes. He didn't get it at the time. At the same time the Lord used that incident to teach me something as well.

I mentioned the incident to a friend of mine who happened to be a former Transit Police Officer. He told me that he experienced the same harassment as a teenager. In his case the officers handcuffed and physically assaulted him.

Shortly after that, as I was driving home from church with my sister sitting in the front passenger seat, I was pulled over for driving through a red light, which I hadn't done. My sister saw that I hadn't run through the red light. She advised me not to argue with the officer but to just do as he asked. As the officer was about to write the ticket he looked across at my sister and questioned what she was holding in her hand. When he noticed the higher ranked law enforcement shield in her hand he jumped back and said, "Sir, next time be careful," and then walked away. Had she have been sitting in the back seat she might not have seen that I had actually driven legally through a green traffic light and not illegally through a red one. At that moment the thought occurred to me that God wants to be right beside me and not somewhere in the backseat of my life. God's position in our lives is very important. One lesson I learned from that incident was; Yes, it's good to have the Lord in your life, but where you have Him in your life is critical.

To make a long story short, my son and I showed up in court. He's my namesake, so when his name was called, we both instinctively stood up to approach the bench. I was suited up for work, sharp tie and all. It's a rarity these days for a young black man to show up in court accompanied by his father. So when the Judge saw me, he didn't know how to deal with me. He assumed that I was the representing Attorney. When the Judge asked if I was an Attorney my son stepped in front of me and said, "He's my father and he's going to take care of this." When the Judge asked the same question again, I had my son step back. Before I could open my mouth, the case was dismissed. I never addressed his questions as to whether or not I was an Attorney. I showed up as my son's father and simply let my Father handle the problem. Don't mess with my son who bears my name. And, that's how God thinks of us - His children.

When I told my son that I would take care of the problem, he never worried about it. I walked into that courtroom with the confidence that my

Heavenly Father was going to take care of the problem for me, and my son was confident that I was going to take care of it for him. A father's presence is critical. Our involvement develops confidence and our absence creates a void.

Just like God with His children, it feels really good that I can do for my children. They're both Christians now. I am now their brother in Christ in addition to being their father. I encourage them in their walk with the Lord. And just as when they were little, I remain in prayer for them.

A father's relationship with his children is vital to their total wellbeing.

Toney Designz
ToneyDesignz@yahoo.com

PRESENCE

Oliver R. Ratney

My father showed me that a man who is dedicated to the wellbeing of his children exemplifies an authentic characteristic of manhood. He showed me that a man is one who is present in the lives of his children.

My dad was a hardworking dedicated man. He held down a couple of jobs, in addition to being a single father for most of my formative years. He made sure that he provided for the family. (I get my work ethic from him.) He was intentional about creating memorable experiences with and for us. That's why I can say without hesitation that I enjoyed my childhood with him.

He took us to different places to see different things. He'd take me to the Cubs and White Sox games, and to football games. We went to basketball games, to auto shows, and all that kind of stuff. I do the same with my kids, to show them that there's more to life than being glued to a computer.

There was no one like him. My father had a presence that commanded respect, one that made you straighten up quick. He wasn't super strict, but he meant business. When I did wrong, I paid the price. For the most part and because of him, I was wise enough not to chase trouble or bow to peer pressure. I knew what he could do, and I didn't want to incur the wrath. Like I said, he was a presence. He was more of a threat than the gang. If I even thought to entertain gang life, I'd have been more afraid of dealing with him than with anyone out in the street. Without too many words, he made sure I knew it.

I'm not too concerned about my teenagers getting involved in gang life. My interaction with them really doesn't leave room for it. I try to stay close to them, so I know what they're doing. I want to make sure that they're not out in the streets up to no good. Like my dad, I'm a presence to reckon with. I can't control what they're going to do with their lives, but I don't want them coming back saying that my absence provoked them to choose adverse lifestyles. If they go out and get involved in that stuff later in life, my conscience is clean. I never provided that kind of influence.

My father's demeanor sort of carried over to me, except that I'm probably more of a disciplinarian than he was. It's not that I was trying to imitate him. I just unconsciously caught some of his attributes. For example, guys that were looking at any one of my sisters were just as intimidated by me as they were by him.

My dad's primary focus was to make sure that we were provided for – food, clothing, roof over our heads, and positive experiences.

He wasn't always involved as much as I would have liked, but he was the pillar of strength, the stability, and the father that we needed. More importantly, we knew he loved us.

I do my best to be active in my kids' lives so that I'm not simply the bread winner. This helps us to bond and remain close. At work I've been known to turn down opportunities so that I could spend time with my kids. The guys at work jokingly tell me that my kids are going to grow up and hate me anyway. I don't think so. We have a relationship.

My father's faith in God: He was always in the church. At the time I didn't know how serious he was. I used to think that my mother was the more serious one. Later in life I realized that his faith shaped his life also. He didn't force me into faith, but he was the one who introduced me to faith in God. I remember Sunday mornings he would get up for church and ask me if I was going. He had done his job of introducing me to the Lord and he knew that I had come to the place where I had to choose the Lord for myself. I watched my father, and I saw that he was active in the church. Hence, here I am today.

I really wasn't all that outgoing when I was growing up. My dad would sign me up for different sports and activities, but his work schedule prohibited him from doing much more than that. I'd try my hand at the extracurricular activities, but then I'd give up if the challenge became uncomfortable. I lacked confidence mainly because I didn't have anyone to encourage me to push past the uncomfortable that came with learning a sport or instrument. My mother was a single mom, working and raising my sisters. My dad raised me and worked long hours to take make sure that we were all taken care of. He did, however, make it a point to participate with me in Boy Scouts.

Today as a father, I encourage my kids to push themselves. I am intentionally active in their lives, to help build their confidence. I try to be hands-on, and I see the difference my presence makes when I help coach them. If they're playing baseball, I put my glove on and throw the ball with them. My presence gives them another reason to strive for excellence. (My eldest son plays a lot better than I did at his age.) With my daughters, I showed up to their dance recitals and to most every other event they were in. Of course, I missed a few, but I did my best to be present. In doing so, I was helping to build their confidence. I want my kids to know that I'm genuinely interested in what they're doing.

Like most teenagers, I went through a know-it-all 'I-got-this' phase. And then, I matured into the realization that I don't know everything and my dad was actually wiser than I was. My eldest son is starting to smell himself, so I'm starting to experience a little bit of that teenage push-back from him. I try to teach him to do things efficiently the first time, so he won't have to keep correcting his mistakes like I did at his age. I'm trying to teach him what my dad taught me, "Don't half-way do a thing. Listen up, it'll help you do it right." I hope I'm teaching my kids to put forth their best effort and to do things properly, decently and in order. Anything less is a poor reflection of who they are.

The example I set matters. I just hope they're watching what goes on in our home between their mom and I. We want them to see how a man and woman are supposed to treat each other, and how they are supposed to carry themselves. I hope my sons pick up on the example their mother has shown them, so they don't pick up the first thing they see in a skirt.

I never smoked or did drugs. Since I've been married, I don't drink. None of those kinds of influences can they ever pin on me. I don't curse. I don't beat my wife. I don't hang out in the street chasing women. My marriage is important to me, foremost because marriage is important to God.

It really is the presence of God in my life that keeps me. With God's help I strive to make my marriage the best that it can be. I try to show my kids that marriage is a good and honorable thing. It's hard work sometimes, but we persevere and get through it. I can comfortably say to my sons, "I showed you how to maintain a loving marriage. So, if you choose to go out and do other things like mess around from woman to woman, you didn't get that from me."

I hope the same for my daughters when it comes to men. My eldest daughter married a man who possesses qualities that she saw demonstrated in our household. I'm honored that she found a man that reminds her of me. Trust me; it really is God's presence that is making all the difference in my kids and in our home.

My dad handed me the mantle of manhood, and then I went further than he went. I want my kids to go even further than I will go. I want them to grow up and have families of their own, to do better for their own families than I did for them. If they do that, then I have accomplished something as a man.

Toney Designz
ToneyDesignz@yahoo.com

I started to see the different layers of stuff that I had accumulated in my life. God became my strength, and by His strength I was able to break old habits and develop new ones - good ones that pleased Him.

IDENTITY

KIPLON TAYLOR

We are pressed on every side by troubles, but we are not crushed. We are perplexed, but not driven to despair. We are hunted down, but never abandoned by God. We get knocked down, but we are not destroyed.
II Corinthians 4:8, 9 (NLT)

"Life for me ain't been no crystal stair." The reality of these words penned by Langston Hughes rang all too true for me in my formative years. I had a mother who most often acted as if she didn't want or love me, an apathetic father who lived his own life away from me, a grandmother who frequently treated me as if I were a bother to her, and a step-

131

grandfather who was the only one to attempt to guide me. My paternal grandfather never acknowledged me as his grandchild, and my mother's husband tried to kick me out to the streets. In short, I was born into a tragically impaired environment and a family riddled with dysfunction. Through it all God never took his eyes off me. In spite of my broken state and because of His unyielding love, God rescued me and placed me on a new path.

When I was born my mother was just fifteen years of age and my father was eighteen. My father acknowledged me, but he seldom came around. My mom and I lived with my step-grandfather James Lacey and my grandmother who was in her early thirties. My grandmother ruled with an iron fist and she passed those parenting practices to her children. So, my mother, working only with the warped template she'd been handed, didn't know how to love her own three children.

When I turned seven my mother, my baby sister and I moved from my grandparents' home to our own place, where after a short time we got evicted; and subsequently evicted from every other place we lived. We ended up bouncing from place to place, and even back to my grandparents' house from time to time. My father lived in the same city that we bounced around in. In spite of my longing, he had very little to do with me. His absence left a void in my life. In my loneliness I found myself crying a lot.

Our home was one where no one talked to or even recognized the true and living God, except for the occasional Biblical movies we were forced to watch as a means of our connection to God. Somehow I knew I could pray to God. At the age of eight I told God that if He got me out of this way of living that I was not going to live the way we were living when I became an adult. I didn't know what I was going to do or become. I just knew that I wasn't going to live like that. I now know that

God's hand was definitely on my life, though I didn't know it at the time.

In spite of the gaping void that gripped me I was a pretty good student. I excelled in everything I set my mind to. I played the guitar, organ, the drums and the saxophone. I think I had a genius mind, but nobody to help cultivate it. My mother didn't understand me or my drive for accomplishment. She most often discouraged my aspirations. Instead of making the effort to build me up, she'd tear me down. There were even times of humiliation when she'd dress me like a girl; I'm talking heels, stockings, dress, wig, and makeup. And other times I was locked in the closet as a form of punishment.

I'd often find myself fantasizing about a better life as a way of escaping the pains of my childhood. I'd envision myself doing great things. I suppose my imaginative aspirations insulated me from life as I knew it and transported me to that better life. As I endured one disappointment after the next, each disappointment fueled my determination for the better life in my dreams. I had a desire to be something greater than the dictations of my environment.

By the time my little brother came along my mother had three children by three different men, and not one of us had a relationship with our fathers. What we had was a lot of different daddies and 'uncles'. In the absence of a male head of household I was often forced to assume the custodial role of an adult, but then I was told that I wasn't in control. My mom would say, "You ain't running nothin' around here!" Then she'd call me out my name. At the same time, she'd disappear for two to three days on end without notice, leaving me to fend for my 6-year-old sister. Those were scary times for a 10-year-old.

When I was in the eighth grade she eloped with her white boyfriend and moved to Las Vegas for two years, abandoning us in the care of my grandmother who ruled with an excessively cruel and resentful hand. My mother returned two years later only to hand my siblings and I over to foster care. She had found a new life that she refused to share with us.

I can go on and on about the painfully unwarranted misfortunes of my life and the anger that gripped me, but I'd rather share what God did for me. He changed me and gave me a new life. He filled the aching void that I had, and He placed me on His path of victory.

After a turn of events, I ended up by my father's place where my younger brother and his mother also lived. He eventually took me to stay with his mother and step-father who was a Pastor. It was there that I was introduced to God. I accepted Jesus Christ as my Savior, and He did just that. He saved me. God rescued me from a life of pain and relieved me of the weight of all the wrong that I had endured. By God's grace I also came to know that nothing wrong that I'd done could ever again be held against me. I was free and clear of all accusations and of any guilt. I was free to live that better life, which has become far better than I'd envisioned as a boy.

I wish I could say that life has been perfect from that point on and that I've become the perfect Christian, but the road ahead had and still has bumps on it. The difference between then and now is that I maneuver the road with God as my navigator and with the confidence that He's got my back.

From experience I know that it's imperative for a young man, or old man for that matter, to know God personally if he's going to be safe in this world. This reality is what I share with young men today.

Today I tell young men that they can find their masculine identity in God. They don't have to go to the streets. They don't have to submit to a gang. If you want to talk 'keeping it real'; the real deal is; the form of masculinity offered by the gangs is nothing but a counterfeit.

In my search for identity I tried gang life. I was a Vice Lord. I flew my colors. Like most young men, I didn't have a clue what I was getting into. I just wanted to belong. All I wanted to know was that somebody cared about me. The love and acceptance I was looking for couldn't be found in the gang. I found it in God.

How does one even know what love is if he's never had it? I hadn't experienced authentic love. What I had was a crippled counterfeit that bore no resemblance to real love. But God! He welcomed me with His authentic love.

If you really want love you have to seek the true source of love, and that's God. Love equips. It does not destroy or tear down. Love provides. Love protects. Love is kind. Love is caring.

God's love showed me that I'm more important than what people made me out to be. I had to come to realize that what I experienced in the past wasn't love. Those things were meant to destroy me, but God turned them around for my good. And because it was God alone who turned my life around, only He can take the credit for the new life that I now enjoy.

What I say to mothers, especially single mothers, is this: Mothers do not emasculate your son. Let him be a man. Teach him that he is a man. Tell him what a man is supposed to do. Tell him how to treat a woman and how to provide for the woman. Tell him what's necessary to be the provider, i.e. integrity, education, a good living. Build your son up with your words. Don't tear him down. Death and life are in the power of the tongue. (Proverbs 18:21) You can speak life over him or death. He's in your influence. He's listening to you. He's watching you. Encourage him to become and support him as much as you can as he becomes. If you don't, then somebody else will speak into his life, and they just might speak the wrong thing.

Let him cry. He's learning, so let him be a boy. Let him go out and be a rough house. Let him play sports. He's a man. Do not weaken or feminize his manhood. Teach him how to manage money. Teach him that money is a tool.

Most importantly, teach him God's word. Make the Bible his foundation for manhood. In doing so, your son will be a phenomenal man. And through it all God will never take his eyes off your son. Despite any brokenness, God's unyielding love will shape your son's life and place him on the path of successful manhood.

MAN-CHILD

Dear God,

Thank You for my little bundle, my baby boy, this Man-child. Once a figment of my imagination, he's now the realization of my many dreams. He's everything and more than I could ever have imagined. What a beautiful child, my baby. He's resting now, swaddled in my embrace, clinging to my nourishment, and wrapped in the warmth of my comfort. My index finger is enclosed in the strength of his tiny hand as he holds my gaze in his own. Or, is it his gaze being held by mine? I'm not sure, but either way I'm captivated by the essence of who he is and by what he is destined to become.

His eyes, so engaging, fade behind the weight of heavy eyelids as if someone has drawn the shades to veil the setting sun. The cadence of his breathing steadies as he falls asleep. I enjoy listening to the rising whisper of his infantile snore, and I welcome the scent of his warm ambrosial breath. This quiet time to play in his brand-new cottony head of curls is my purest delight. Everything about him is tender and new. God, this demanding yet uncomplicated little person is so easy to please. I love him. Thank You.

I'm amazed that at this very moment in time I coddle a solitary life called my son. Though he's my son, he's far more than just my son. He's progenitor of generations to come. I hold someone's father, grandfather, great, and great-great grandfather. I hold multiple generations all wrapped up in his tender loins. I sit here smiling into the eyes of today and tomorrow at the same time. Something tells me that tucked in the center of my embrace is the embodiment of greatness. Something tells me that today I hold tomorrow's benefit.

God, I know he's Your child and that he's simply here on loan to me. But who is this little yet significant person that I waited for with unreserved expectancy, and now wait on as if he were emperor or king? Who is this that I am so privileged to hold in the fold of my arms, to play with, nourish and adore? Who is this little person that possesses a full-size soul and boundless potential? I often remind myself that the only thing little about my bundle is the size of his body, and that but for a moment. Before I know it, he will be the embodiment of a mature man.

This budding and purpose-filled man-child has captivated my ever-growing devotion with the waking of each day. So, who is he and what will he become? Who is it really that I'm holding today?

This man-child's fascinating existence at this juncture in history is no mere accident. I know that he is here on purpose for a purpose. Without a doubt, I hold in my arms a noteworthy individual, one the world is soon to realize.

Tell me, am I holding a time-wised sage, scribe, or world-renowned poet? Do I hold a lexicographer, a master linguist, or multilingual translator? Is he a world-class doctor or first-rate geneticist? Is he the one to discover answers to age old queries about DNA, RNA, and their non-coding sequences? Is he the one to finally find and develop the cure for sickle cell disease, or for genetically dominant diseases like Huntington's disease? Is he the scientist to break the code to cancers' malignancy or unearth Your remedy to end AIDS' global plague? I don't know yet, but I'm certain that I'm holding a great man.

God, is he the Astrophysicist or Aerospace Engineer who will calculate the position of newfound planets or even invent next generation spacecraft for interplanetary navigation? Is he the Architect to design buildings to house Planetary Scientists across the lunar landscape? Is he the Seismologist to develop the most precise seismometers and accelerometers to accurately forecast as never before the earth's quakes and shifts of its tectonic plates? Is he the one to re-engineer the way in which we fuel automobiles and the manner in which we travel? Or, will he be the world leader renowned for successfully negotiating peace in lands ravaged by war?

He's my beautiful baby, and his mere presence has tenderized my heart. I wish that I could protect him from all of life's ills. Like any mother, I wish to be sure that no one will ever hurt him in any way. I'd do my best to disinfect his world and place him in a sterile, pristine and problem free environment suitable just for him. I'd even go before him to shield him from life's difficulty and misfortune. If I could repel inevitable pain to keep him from ever being hurt, I'd consider that too. But wisdom tells me that I would only be protecting him from success.

So, through each trial strengthen him. You be his buttress when fierce storms come to knock him down. Take the pain that life will throw his way and use it to inoculate him from unnecessary woes. Help him to recognize and relate to You early in life. Help him as he makes up his mind at each of life's crossroads. With You as his guide he'll choose right over wrong. May he always stand firm living an unapologetic life of integrity. May he forever walk in Your abounding favor.

Protect him, Lord. You be his continued defense, so that he's never standing alone. Let him always be aware that he is empowered by You, and that he never has to bow to systemic inequities sanctioned against him. Make him a barrier breaker, a unity maker, and a first-rate negotiator. Place in him the offensive strategy that You designed for him even before his forefathers' conception.

We're enjoying him today. We live with the expectation of an excellent-to-outstanding tomorrow for our man-child.

Architect of Life, shape his character and make him a disciplined man, one who stands on truth and lives by its principles. Tenderize his heart and make him a man of compassion. Help us to form him, so that he's the best according to your intent.

You are a brilliant God, and he was made in Your image. Sharpen his acumen and help him to cultivate his thoughts. Make him a man of reflective thought and a master strategist. Give him the mind to decipher enigmas, and a legacy of wisdom to hand to his children – a legacy that they'll proudly bequeath to their own children.

When people come to tell him he's weak, You be his strength. When danger comes to harm him, You be his security. When accusers come to defame his character, You be his voice. When temptation sneaks up to knock him off course, You straighten his head and steady his gait. When pressure causes him to sink, You be his buttress and keep him upright. You be his stability and his standard. You be the measure by which he aligns himself. You be the love in his heart that initiates his every thought, word, and endeavor. You, God, be his truth.

We ask that You endow him with good health and longevity.

His father stands ready to hand him the blueprint for manhood, so that he's prepared for the realities of masculinity. We stand together to shower our seed with the nurturing and leadership that he will need to not only survive but to thrive.

Giver of Life, You have placed this tender life in our hands. Now we look to You to help us help him to live out Your great plan. This precious man-child is Your man.

In Jesus' name, we say Amen.

Deborah Williams

I SEE A MAN

Deborah Williams

I was out to lunch with three colleagues - one a young British fellow, the other a French woman, and my friend the youngest of us all, a 27'ish Caucasian-American female. As we waited on our meals the four of us observed an eye-catching couple entering the restaurant. In my opinion the couple was ordinary, but perhaps not so ordinary. Let me explain.

The man was a Black man whose commandeering presence caused the couple to stand out. We, as with several other patrons, were captivated by the man's towering well-built athletic physique. In his

151

arms was a preschool aged girl who bore the resemblance of the obviously pregnant woman at his side. This man's presence was so captivating that my initial thought was, "This athletic giant must be balling on one of the city's two NBA teams."

I'll describe this couple to you in more detail. The man looked to be about seven feet tall, dark in complexion with a slender muscular build. He was comfortably dressed in an easy fitting velour jogging suit of the finest quality. He entered the restaurant holding the hand of the well-dressed pregnant woman at his side. The woman was adorned with long loose curls that draped her shoulders. The couple wore matching wedding bands. The child in the man's arms resembled both he and the pregnant woman. Given my observation I thought it quite obvious that they were a family unit; husband and wife - daddy, mommy, child and baby on the way. Oddly enough, this was not so obvious to my colleagues.

Each one of us at the table gave comment about the man. My friend complimented, "He's hot." My boy, the cocksure Brit decreed, "He looks like a criminal." And, even more brazen, the French Madame declared, "He looks like a rapist." When it was my turn to give analysis I said, "I see a man with his family."

What the …??? Yo! Europe what's up? You need to change the lens through which you peep my brother. In spite of the warped image conjured by twisted minds…

When I see my brother, I see
Innocent, not guilty
Benefit and not doubt
Good, not bad
I see Husband, I see Dad.

When I see my brother, I see
An Honest Man, not a con-man
I see Power according to God's ultimate plan.

When I see my brother, I see
Might, not fright
And, I'm not afraid to walk up on him in the dark of night.

When I see my brother, I see
Rich man, Doctor, Lawyer and Family Chief
Not poor-man, not beggar-man, and definitely not
thief.

When I see my brother, I see
Expertise, not ignorance
And Brilliance beyond compare
I see Resilience, and not one given to despair.

When I see my brother, I see
Success, not failure
I see Wisdom and Strength
I see Sagacity at its Best
My God, I see a Man standing shoulders above the
rest.

When I see my brother, I see
A Man who loves his woman
This includes big momma, his mother
His sister, daughter, his wife – lover.

When I see my brother, I see
A Man worth Honorable Mention
A Man who's got my Undivided Attention.

When I see my brother, I see   **a Man**.

BLACK MAN

Deborah Williams

It's been so long now that I can't recall how it all began. What I know for sure is that today I stand tall in spite of the atrocities that have beset me, and I stand as a result of my fortitude. I'd be a fool to take all the credit, because I definitely recognize that were it not for God, I'd have neither fortitude nor courage to excel past my pain. Though ever so excruciating, and of course I often question why, I know that it's God who navigates my course. The other day you asked me, "Who do you think you are? Where'd you come from, and where do you think you're going?" It's to this end that I stand here today to address your query. Let me start from as far back as I can recall. I'll bring you up to speed, so I can take you into my – no, our tomorrow. Because, as neighbors in America and cohabitants of this globe, your very own destiny is inextricably tied to mine.

Some years ago, I was snatched from my family and sold for little of nothing to a band of strange men who spoke in a foreign tongue. I was bartered for mixed goods, fire-arms, and ammunition. These hostile criminals took me in chains to a dungeon-like fort along the western shore. They abused and beat me before shoving my blistered and chained body down into a ship's dank murky hold. Guilty of no crime, I lay shackled, agonizing in the cramped putrid quarters of the ship's bowels. Any attempt to free myself or to fight back was met with malicious and often lethal blows from my kidnappers.

I filled the ships belly as starvation filled mine. My own cry and my questions 'why' echoed over and over again in my ear. Surrounded by the smell of my very own death, I called out to God and to whatever god that would listen but heard no answer. The hollow sound of abandonment resounded louder in my heart than the boisterous waves licking the sides of the ship. I don't think I need to tell you that I longed for death with every shove from the billowing waves. When we finally reached the unfamiliar Eastern Shore, I was herded off the ship and placed alongside cattle for sale. And, I was sold.

Doomed, or better said, damned to perennial servitude and deprived of my personal freedom, I slaved for these strange speaking criminals from dawn to dusk year after year. I went from providing for my family back home on the other side of this nightmare, to eating animal entrails and rancid table scraps. I went from being esteemed for my strength to being disdained and beaten for my might. I once walked proud in my intellectual prowess and physical vigor, but life's perilous twist caused me to question why God had endowed me with such potency, only to be derisively exploited by these green-eyed captors.

I was treated as a savage by the savage himself. They, both he and she, beat and bludgeoned me, violated and raped me, forced me to breed and then tore me from my children. Yet, I was the savage. Stripped, I was stripped of everything I proudly called my own; stripped of my name and language, my home and family, my culture and customs, my history and legacy, my heritage and birthright. Oh, but they gave me something, yes they did. They gave me their surnames and a glimpse of the wealth that my sweat and blood earned for them. In their arrogance, they even believed that they were doing me a favor.

Let me pause for a moment. Talking about this is conjuring up some negative feelings, that'll only cause me to veer from the purpose of this discourse.

Thanks for bearing with me. I'll continue now.

I labored every day but Sundays, usually. Sunday was the day that all 'good folk' went to church. So, the 'good folk', they went to church and summoned me to church as well. The paradox of the day was that the 'good folk' committed hellish crimes against me all week, but on Sundays they sat with all piety before God, as if they themselves manufactured righteousness.

Relegated to congregating in the church yard and sometimes inside the rear of the building when permitted, I'd listen to the 'good folk' worship, and I too would often worship. I'd listen to the 'good man' preach from the Bible. All too often I was perplexed by a message that either conflicted with his way of life or propagated his odious deeds. But because I was forbidden to read his language and had no Bible in my own tongue in this foreign land, I was consigned to a distorted gospel; that is, until I learned to read his words.

Learning to read the language of the land was the defining moment in my destiny. It was then that the light came on bringing closure to the Dark Ages. Much like the repercussion in Europe initiated by Martin Luther's protest against his contemporary Piety, the illumination instigated my longing for information and simultaneously ignited the wrath of my captors. When the light came on, I learned from the very same Bible that "There is no respect of persons with God." I examined the Scripture for myself and received confirmation that I am a favored child of the Almighty, causing me to stand erect as the man that I am.

The rising illumination caused my ears to resonate with the sound of insurrection from my brother in the Sugar Islands. It awakened me to Dutty Boukman's call to revolution that ignited the World War that culminated in the emancipation of my brother in Saint-Domingue. It moved me to act on my longing for freedom and equipped me with the dexterity to claim my human entitlement.

I eventually spent Sundays in my own services worshiping in a manner familiar only to me. I sang, danced, shouted and cried out to God. I beat my tambourine, slapped my thigh, stamped my feet, and hummed just about every Sunday. When my song carried over into the week, I hummed and sang hymns of freedom while I worked. Though I sang in his language, he hadn't a clue of my words. He thought me to be ignorant. But, in his very own ignorance he mistook my song for rhythmic banter, when the song I sang was far more sophisticated and cryptic than he'd ever imagined. In fact, its encryption was as covert as any algorithmic code, securing a message solely for its intended recipient.

Like my brother in the isles of the Caribbean Sea, I sought to be free. On one day, I'd take the route of 'by any means necessary' and face venomous force. On another, I'd bow my knee praying for some sort of divine or benevolent rescue. And yet, on another day I'd wonder if Wilberforce would cross the ocean and protest for even me.

When Emancipation Day came, I was uncertain of my feelings. Exultant though I was, what would I do and how was I to live outside of this manacled existence? I'd been imprisoned for more than three and a half consecutive life sentences, and consequently forgot much of what freedom tasted like. But as any man would do, I stepped out into freedom, in search of independence and all that it embodies.

With courage pounding in my chest, relief on my back, and the currency in my pocket – my mother's prayers, I got up and walked out of slavery past the dogs that he unleashed on me to tear my flesh. I walked past nooses purposely sanctioned for the breaking of my neck. I pushed my way through the bone crushing force of his water cannons. I stepped over the debris left in the wake of bombs that he hurled through my windows. I walked out of the fires that he ignited to annihilate me. I made it through that wretched day that he beat the breath from my youthful lungs because I but whistled. Till...even the world felt the pain of my mutilated body. I walked forward with hand in pocket clasping my change, knowing that I'd need it in order to make a dollar out of fifteen cents.

Now I stand before you today, an accomplished man with far more yet to achieve. I stand as a man historically beaten, but perpetually undefeated. I walk as a man hindered but unstopped. In spite of his extrajudicial bullets that penetrate my back, I live as a man excelling in all that I undertake. I rise. And as I rise in my Father's strength, I lift my siblings and my mother, and I honor my Father.

Don't stand on the sidelines gazing. Get in sync or be swept away in the wake of my success. Walk with me, for my quest is excellence. Work with me, and let us celebrate ground-breaking exploits and noble feats together. Kneel alongside me, and fill your own pocket with the divine currency that has sustained and still propels me. But waste time begrudging me, and I'll simply watch you in life's rear-view mirror as I continue to innovate, develop, and create.

So, you want to know who I am? You ask my name and deliberate my accomplishment. There's plenty time left for roll call.

Front and Center:

<u>Inventors</u>

Internet Visionary Emmit McHenry
Creator of the .com

Gladys West, Ph.D
Mathematician, a pioneer of Global Positioning
System (GPS) Technology, Inductee into the Air
Force Space and Missile Pioneers Hall of Fame

Philip Emeagwali, Ph.D
Inventor of the World's Fastest Computer

Iddris Sandu
Tech Wunderkind, recipient of the Presidential
Scholar Award from President Barack Obama,
Cultural Architect, Software Engineer, Technology
Design Architect, Co-creator of the world's first
smart retail store experience –
The Marathon Store

Silas Adekunle
Robotics Engineer, Inventor,
Developer of the world's first gaming robot
Founder and CEO of Reach Robotics

Lonnie G. Johnson
Inventor, Thermoelectric Energy Converter

Lisa Gelobter
Computer Scientist, Technologist and Chief
Executive, Developer of several internet
technologies, including Shockwave Flash,
Animated GIFs

Veloris Sonny Marshall
Inventor, Founder / CEO / President of Marshall
Communications, Lieutenant Colonel United States
Air Force

Marie Ban Brittan Brown
Inventor, Home Security System -
Closed-Circuit Television Security

Marian R. Croak
Inventor, Voice over Internet Protocol (VoIP)
Networks, Holds over 200 patents

Gerald Anderson "Jerry" Lawson
Electronic Engineer, Designer of the Fairchild
Channel F Video Game Console, Pioneer of the
Commercial Video Game Cartridge

Ivan Yaeger
Inventor, Yaeger Prosthetic Arm (prosthetic arm
controlled through activating sensors on the
human body)

James McLurkin, Ph.D.
Robotics Engineer

Marc Regis Hannah, Ph.D.
Electrical Engineer, Computer Graphics Designer

Maurice Ashley
International Chess Grandmaster,
App Designer, Puzzle Inventor

James Edward Maceo West
Inventor and Acoustician, Co-inventor of the foil
electric microphone and the silicon microphone,
holds 250+ foreign and U.S. patents for the
production and design of microphones and
techniques for creating polymer foil electrets.

Fathia Abdullah
At age 12, Inventor of laundry folding robot

Scientists

Shirley Ann Jackson, Ph.D.
Theoretical Physicist, Chairperson of the U.S.
Nuclear Regulatory Commission and 18th President
of Rensselaer Polytechnic Institute

Carlos Handy, Ph.D.
Physicist

Estella Atekwana, Ph.D.
Geophysicist

Agnes A. Day, Ph.D.
Microbiologist

Stephon Alexander, Ph.D.
Theoretical Physicist, Cosmologist, Musician

Homer Alfred Neal, Ph.D.
Particle Physicist, Professor

Gregory S. Jenkins, Ph.D.
Atmospheric Scientist

Darnell Eugene Diggs, Ph.D.
Research Physicist

Lafayette Frederick, Ph.D.
Botanist

Linneaus C. Dorman, Ph.D.
Organic Chemist, Inventor

Georgia Mae Dunston, Ph.D.
Geneticist

George Robert Carruthers, Ph.D.
Astrophysicist

Gibor Basri Ph.D.
Astrophysicist, Physics Professor

Winston Anderson, Ph.D.
Biomedical Scientist

Jesse Ernest Wilkins Jr., Ph.D.
Nuclear Scientist, Mechanical Engineer,
Mathematician; Developed mathematical models
to explain gamma radiation

Albert Antoine, Ph.D.
Chemist, Chemistry Professor

Lilia Ann Abron, Ph.D.
Chief Executive Officer and Chemical Engineer

Ketevi Adikle Assamagan, Ph.D.
Physicist, Brookhaven National Laboratory
Co-founder, African School of Fundamental
Physics and Applications,
www.africanschoolofphysics.org

Erich D. Jarvis, Ph.D.
Neurobiologist

Diola Bagayoko Ph.D.
Scientist and Educator

Frederic Bertley Ph.D.
Immunologist, Health Researcher, Museum
President

Warren M. Washington, Ph.D.
Atmospheric Scientist, Senior Scientist in the
Climate Change Research Section in the Climate
and Global Dynamics Division, National Center for
Atmospheric Research

William M. Jackson, Ph.D.
Chemist, Research Scientist (photochemistry, lasers
chemistry, astrochemistry)

Esther Arvilla Harrison Hopkins, Ph.D., J.D.
Chemist, Patent Attorney

Randolph W. Bromery, Ph.D.
Geologist, Educator

Lloyd Noel Ferguson, Ph.D.
Chemist, Author and Educator

Odest Chadwicke Jenkins, Ph.D.
Computer Scientist, Robotics Engineer

Marian Cecelia Johnson-Thompson, Ph.D.
Molecular Virologist, Educator

Ralph Etienne-Cummings, Ph.D.
Electrical Engineer, Computer Scientist, Professor

Evan B. Forde
Oceanographer

Essex E. Finney, Ph.D.
Agricultural Engineer

Pamela J. Gunter-Smith, Ph.D.
Physiologist, University President

Sossina Haile, Ph.D.
Chemical Engineer

Aprille Ericsson-Jackson, Ph.D.
Aerospace Engineer

Wesley L. Harris, Ph.D.
Aerospace Engineer

Dr. Bruce Ovbiagele
Vascular Neurologist

Astronauts

Michael Anderson, Ph.D.
Aerospace Engineer, Staff Development Engineer,
Branch Chief of the Air Force Flight Dynamics
Laboratory

Guion S. Bluford, Jr., Ph.D.
Aerospace Engineer, U.S. Air Force Officer, Fighter
Pilot, Astronaut

Charles F. Bolden, Jr.
NASA Administrator, United States Marine Corps
Major General, Astronaut

Colonel Yvonne Darlene Cagle, M.D.
U.S. Air Force Colonel Flight Surgeon, Scientist,
Educator, Astronaut

Colonel Benjamin Alvin Drew
Retired United States Air Force Colonel, Astronaut

Jeanette J. Epps, Ph.D.
Aerospace Engineer, Astronaut

Victor J. Glover, Jr.
Commander United States Navy, Astronaut

Frederick D. Gregory
Astronaut, NASA's Deputy Administrator
(confirmed 2002), former United States Air Force
Pilot, Military Engineer, Test Pilot

Bernard Anthony Harris Jr., M.D.
Physician, Astronaut

Joan Higginbotham
Astronaut

Mae C. Jemison, M.D.
Physician, Astronaut

Ronald E. McNair, Ph.D.
Astronaut, Physicist

Leland D. Melvin
NFL Draft pick - Detroit Lions, Wide Receiver,
Astronaut

Robert Lee Satcher, Jr., M.D., Ph.D.
Orthopedic Surgeon, Chemical Engineer,
Astronaut

Winston E. Scott
Astronaut, Executive Director of the Florida Space
Authority

Stephanie D. Wilson
Astronaut Veteran of three spaceflights

Robert L. Curbeam, Jr.
Captain, US Navy and National Aeronautics and
Former NASA Astronaut, United States Navy
Captain

U.S. Military

William E. "Kip" Ward,
United States Army Four-star General, served as
Commander, U.S. Africa Command (AFRICOM)

Brigadier General Lorna Mahlock
Director, Command, Control, Communications
and Computers (C4) and the Deputy Department
of the U.S. Navy Chief Information Officer (CIO) of
the Marine Corps

General Colin L. Powell
12th Chairman of the Joint Chiefs of Staff,
U.S. Secretary of State, National Security Advisor,
United States Army 4-Star General

Clergy

Eric D. Thomas, Ph.D. (ETTheHipHopPreacher)
Pastor, Motivational Speaker, Author, Businessman

Bishop T.D. Jakes
Executive Pastor at The Potter's House, CEO, Movie
Mogul, Businessman, Author

The Honorable Minister Louis Farrakhan
Leader of the Nation of Islam

Dr. Myles Munroe
Pastor, Evangelist, Professor, Speaker,
Businessman, Leadership Consultant to Heads of
States

Bishop Charles E. Blake, Sr.
Bishop of the Church of God in Christ
President of the Pan African Children's Fund /
Save Africa's Children

Rev. A. R. Bernard
Pastor, Author, Businessman, President of the
Council of Churches of the City of New York

Statesmen

Dr. Condoleezza Rice
Sixty-sixth United States Secretary of State; former
National Security Advisor to the 43rd U.S.
President, formerly the Provost (the Chief Budget
and Academic Officer) of Stanford University

Mayor Svante L. Myrick
Mayor of Ithaca, New York (at age 25)

President Barack Hussein Obama II
44th President of the United States of America

Physicians

Dr. Shawna Nesbitt, M.D.
Cardiovascular Scientist, Cardiovascular Physician

Dr. Mahoney Jean Williams, M.D.
Emergency Medicine Physician, Washington, DC

Dr. Ada Cooper, J.D., D.D.S.
Lawyer, Dentist

Dr. Patricia Bath, M.D.
Ophthalmologist, Inventor, Humanitarian, and
Academic, Co-founder of the American Institute
for the Prevention of Blindness

Dr. Velma P. Scantlebury, M.D.
Associate Director of the Kidney Transplant
Program at Christiana Care Health System

Dr. Oluyinka O. Olutoye, M.D.
Pediatric Surgeon, Co-Director of the Texas
Children's Fetal Center and fetal surgery team
member, Professor of Surgery, Pediatrics, and
Obstetrics

Dr. Benjamin S. Carson, Sr., M.D.
Director of Pediatric Neurosurgery at Johns
Hopkins Hospital in Maryland

Businessmen/Women

Gwen and Brandy Hambrick
Founders of Future World Productions –
Cincinnati, Ohio, Youth Arts & Leadership
Academy

LeBron R. James Sr.
CEO, Philanthropist, Master Strategist, Professional
Basketball Player

Uchendi "Chin" Nwani,
Millionaire Ex-Convict, Author, Owner of the
nation's largest barber college

Writer

Ta-Nehisi Coates
Prolific Writer, Published Author, Journalist,
National Correspondent at The Atlantic, National
Book Award for Nonfiction Recipient; New York
University's Arthur L. Carter Journalism Institute,
Distinguished Writer in Residence

Musician

James White
Dove, Stellar, and GMWA award winning
Producer, Composer, Arranger and Musician,
Vocal Director, Executive Director of Music and
Worship Arts, *Sunday Service* Choir Director of
The Samples Gospel Choir,

Dedicated Family Man & Loving Husband

Derrick Barnes
Husband, Father of Four, Soccer Dad
Drexel University Graduate, Structural and Civil
Engineer, Percussionist

This list includes your name and millions more!

> **If you're going to be here, you may as well change the world.**

CONCLUSION

Freddie Williams

There is an adage that says a child without a father is like a house without a roof. Envision your own home with all of your possessions inside. Now, remove the roof. This seems like a harmless scenario, until a storm comes. In the absence of a roof your possessions are susceptible to damage and destruction. A fatherless child is no different than a roofless house, uncovered and vulnerable to any and all outside forces. Without the stabilizing covering of a father the internal makeup of generations after generation of uncovered youth is being adversely impacted by direct hits from storms, i.e. societal malevolence.

Allow me to speak to you of a man named Mephibosheth[1]. Mephibosheth was the son of a prince. Royalty was in his lineage. Kingship coursed through his veins. At the tender age of 5, Mephibosheth, in the absence of his father, was dropped and subsequently crippled by the person who was entrusted with his care. How many like Mephibosheth have been mishandled, misled, and misplaced by the very person(s) charged with caring for them; and like Mephibosheth, left incapacitated limping through life because of childhood trauma? Through the course of events and by no fault of his own, he who was once destined for the throne was found living as a pauper in the house of a servant in a place called Lodebar.

Literally translated, Lodebar means no communication or no word. But a simple play on words says that because of what occurred in his childhood, he had lowered-the-bar in his adulthood. Anytime we lower the bar, we reduce the standards, decrease the criteria, and adulterate the prerequisites and process. Anytime we operate from a place that is contingent upon watered down standards it is inevitable that lives will be adversely affected. In basketball, the standard calls for a basket set at a height of 10 feet. A person executing 360° windmill dunks on a 6-foot basket is completely unimpressive. Why? The lowered bar is far below the inspiring standard.

Black man, you have a rich, robust, royal bloodline. Have you lived up to your potential, your power, and the realization of your purpose? Or, are you, because of your childhood, merely existing rather than living, and surviving as opposed to thriving?

There's a biblical account in the book of Joshua where decades after being liberated from Egypt, the Israelites were on the brink of entering the Promised Land and seizing their God appointed inheritance, only to be confronted with the staggering realization that they had breached Abrahamic covenant due to their failure to circumcise. While innocuous to most, circumcision was a condition of covenant that required fathers to ensure the circumcision of their sons on the 8th day of the child's life. This single obligatory act connected the child to his culture, his identity, his future, and his God. At the time of revelation each one of these Israelite men, all over twenty years of age, had to be circumcised in order to move forward. No doubt you understand that a circumcision is easily endured and forgotten at eight days of age but is excruciating and traumatic at twenty years old. After the men get circumcised, the Bible says the Lord commanded them to heal before they went into the Promised Land. Hurt people cannot handle the inheritance. Hurting people inevitably hinder and curtail the process that qualifies them for the promise.

Similarly, for us there are fundamental actions and pivotal lessons in each male's personal journey into destiny, without which he cannot advance. This is a rite of passage that should have been bestowed on us by our fathers during the formative years, but for many never transpired due to negligence, oversight, ignorance, or the absence of our fathers.

This biblical parallel is significant, for from the depth of these pages that you are surely compelled to reread, you will hear a resounding clarion call for healing. Many have moved into adult situations without the necessary guidance, instruction, and input that should have been bestowed upon us in childhood. We are a nation of hurting men raising children and transferring our pains, problems, and hang-ups to the next generation. Ignorance, while it is a private decision, has public consequences. Be it involuntary or willful, ignorance is transferable and can become multigenerational. The Israelite men were at a standstill because of the negligence of the generation of the men before them. A key to raising a boy to manhood and a girl to womanhood is being keenly aware of the didactic moments which will prepare, equip, and empower him and her to succeed. To quote Franklin D. Roosevelt, "We cannot always build the future for our youth, but we can build our youth for the future."

I was stricken by one of the chapters in which the brother conveyed that his father was present as a provider, a protector, and model of manhood. He mentioned that his father passed on to him wise advice. But as he emerged into adulthood, he found himself manifesting not what his father taught, but what he caught from his father. In reading I was reminded of James Baldwin's statement, "Children have never been very good at listening to their elders, but have never failed to imitate them". It impressed this upon me: Minds are changed, shaped, and formed more through observation than through argument. It is what we do that is indelibly imprinted upon the minds and hearts of our youth.

PROCESS is a word that coursed through each man's discourse. Manhood, the obtaining of such is not an event but a process. As I read and examined my life and black lives, I questioned, have we lowered the bar and forsaken the process for the product? Any manufacturer will inform you that their focus is on the process and not product. When the process is exacting, definite, and thorough, the quality of the product is guaranteed. We unconsciously forgo process when we tell 6-year olds they are the man of the house, when we ardently declare to 10-year olds to suck it up and be a man; when adult loads, burdens, weights, and cares are placed on the delicate shoulders of youth. Process. The progression of a man-child arriving into manhood ensures that upon arrival his foundation is sound, marked by integrity, balanced, and authentic.

Crimes involving counterfeit money are handled by the Secret Service. Each agent, via an arduous training process, is equipped with the capacity and expertise to scrutinize and identify counterfeit money almost without fail. An agent's level of exactness is obtained not by the study and examination of the counterfeit, but by the continued exposure of and to the authentic. By becoming intimately familiar with every facet, nuance, aspect, and quality of the authentic article, the fake sticks out like a sore thumb.

The unfortunate truth is that throughout the course of our lives the majority of us have been exposed to counterfeit examples of manhood. Whether propagated by media or misguided males, by sports, the streets or in our homes, whether intentional or accidental, our contact and connection with authentic manhood has been few and far between. This is so pervasive that when actual manhood manifests itself, in ignorance we fail to recognize it, and we consequently malign it. The tragedy here is that we teach what we know and reproduce what we are.

INSUFFICIENT FUNDS

For too long our children have come to make withdrawals from us, only to find us bankrupt and bereft of what they require. The receipt for their request has been INSUFFICIENT FUNDS. Our children are forced to leave us unfulfilled, unfed, and unfueled, only to find a warped similitude of what they're looking for in illicit sources. They have come to us for guidance, but for too long we've put the cart before the horse and majored in the minors. To our generational demise we've been overly concerned with what we're leaving TO our children materially instead of what we are leaving IN them spiritually, ideologically, intellectually, and morally.

As you turn the final page of the last chapter of this book, let it symbolically close any chapter in your personal life of mediocrity, menial thinking, or marginal living. A blow is being struck certain and sure to the very heart of manhood, and it is reverberating throughout our nation and recoiling upon our children.

Men, let's recalibrate and shift our children in the right direction…in the way that they should go.

[1]Mephibosheth: 2 Samuel 4:4; 2 Samuel 9

Malachi 4:6

And He shall turn the heart of the fathers to the children, and the heart of the children to their fathers…

Proverbs 13:22

A good man leaves an inheritance to his children's children …

Proverbs 17:6

Children's children are the crown of old men; and the glory of children are their fathers.

Ephesians 6:10-17

Be strong in the Lord and in his mighty power. Put on all of God's armor so that you will be able to stand firm against all strategies of the devil. For we are not fighting against flesh-and-blood enemies, but against evil rulers and authorities of the unseen world, against mighty powers in this dark world, and against evil spirits in the heavenly places.

Therefore, put on every piece of God's armor so you will be able to resist the enemy in the time of evil. Then after the battle you will still be standing firm. Stand your ground, putting on the belt of truth and the body armor of God's righteousness. For shoes, put on the peace that comes from the Good News so that you will be fully prepared. In addition to all of these, hold up the shield of faith to stop the fiery arrows of the devil. Put on salvation as your helmet, and take the sword of the Spirit, which is the word of God.

Contributors:

James Bazemore

William Belle

LeMar Connor

Ronald R. Hines

Pastor Craig Holliday

E. Lavar Iverson

Peter Lawson

Antwon E. M.

Oliver R. Ratney

Brother Reginald

Ryan Roberts

Apostle Kiplon Taylor

Alva E. Williams, Jr.

Minister Freddie Williams

Tylik Williams (Varlet Rose)

Emmett for President - the book for boys who strive
for excellence. Available on Amazon.com

Kids **for** *President®*
Children's Book Series

Journal

_____

_____

_____

_____

_____

_____

_____

_____

_____

Made in the USA
Monee, IL
21 June 2021

71859431R00118